MW01147076

SEC Sports Quotes

Over 800 Brief, Brilliant Bursts of Life from Former Coaches, Players and Observers of The Southeastern Conference

Copyright ©2002 by CEW Enterprises
Baton Rouge, Louisiana

All rights reserved. Except for short quotes used in reviews in periodicals, or other media, no portion of this book may be reproduced or transmitted in any form or by any means, electronic or mechanical, including photocopying, recording, or by information storage or retrieval system, without explicit permission by the publisher, CEW Enterprises, P.O. Box 44189, Baton Rouge, LA 70804-4189.

The words and thoughts displayed in this book are not, in all cases, exact quotes, since some have been edited for clarity and pithiness. In every instance the author has tried to communicate the speaker's original intent. In some instances, information from this book was recovered through secondary sources, primarily print media and sports media guides of the schools of the Southeastern Conference. While every effort was made to ensure the accuracy of these sources, the accuracy cannot be guaranteed. For additions, deletions, corrections or clarifications in future printings of this work, please write CEW Enterprises.

Books by CEW Enterprises are available at wholesale discount prices for sales in bulk purchases, SEC Alumni organizational fund-raising, or for educational use. For more information, contact CEW Enterprises at cewarner@sectraditions.com or cewarner@mindspring.com.

Printed in the United States of America
By Moran Printing
Design by Chanler Holden (http://www.barnstormdesigns.com)
Typesetting and Layout by Marla Warner
Edited by Dr. John Hilburn

Dedicated to the fans of the Southeastern Conference.
They are like no others.

Table of Contents

Introduction

The Southeastern Conference, with its rich and storied 69-year history of athletic accomplishments and academic excellence, has perhaps forged the finest tradition of intercollegiate competition of any athletic conference in the United States since its 1933 inception.

Southeastern Conference Sports Quotes is a rich collection of over 800 quotations spoken by many of the SEC's more noteworthy athletes, coaches and observers. This unique amalgam of sporting wit and wisdom typifies the South's deep-rooted fascination and visceral connection with sports and documents for posterity the sometimes inspiring, the sometimes provocative, but always heartfelt, words of the sporting figures that have shaped, and continue to shape, popular culture in the Deep South.

- Chris Warner, May, 2002

"The South—where roots, place, family and tradition are the essence of identity."

- Carl Degler

Alabama

"I thought Tech people drank a better brand of whiskey than this."
> *- Paul "Bear" Bryant, picking up a bottle that was thrown at him from the stands by Georgia Tech fans*

"He literally knocked the door down. I mean right off the hinges. A policeman came in and asked who knocked the door down, and Coach Bryant said, 'I did.' The cop just said, 'Okay' and walked away."
> *- Jerry Duncan, describing an irate Paul Bryant after a 7-7 tie with Tennessee*

"The first thing that I do is get a kicker and a punter. If the kicking game wasn't important they would have called it armball." *- Bear Bryant*

"Bear Bryant left Kentucky because he won the SEC Championship in football and received a cigarette lighter for his efforts. On the flip side, Adolph Rupp won the SEC in basketball and got a Rolls Royce." *- Unknown*

"If you don't like to worry, why do it? It doesn't help your performance." *- Joe Namath*

"Don't ever give up on ability. Don't ever give up on a player that has it." *- Bear Bryant*

"When we won the league championship, all the married guys on the club had to thank their wives for putting up with all the stress and strain all season. I had to thank all the single broads in New York." *- Joe Namath, commenting on his professional playing days*

"Keep your head up; act like a champion." *- Bear Bryant*

"WE BELIEVE THAT ON THE EIGHTH DAY, THE LORD CREATED THE CRIMSON TIDE." *- Alabama Senator Jeremiah Denton*

"If you let one game or one play haunt you, your mind's in the wrong place." *- Kenny Stabler*

"I've been here so long that when I got here, the Dead Sea wasn't even sick."
- Wimp Sanderson, Alabama basketball coach

"The last thing he made us do before the game was get off the bus and put on those old, woolen, hot jerseys." *- Harry Gilmer, former Alabama halfback who played under coach Frank Thomas*

"I like my girls blonde and my Johnny Walker red."
- Joe Namath

"Keep the players high. Make practice a pleasure, not a lark. Be a disciplinarian, but not a slave driver. It's better to have a short, full practice than a long, lazy one."
- *Frank Thomas*

"It was all about the respect factor with me. It was all about P.J. [Carlesimo] disrespecting me as a man. You don't talk to people the way that P.J. talked to me. To have my pride and my respect and my manhood means more than any dollar amount."
- *Latrell Sprewell, 1998, explaining why he choked his Golden State Warrior's coach, P.J. Carlesimo*

"I've seen everybody say everything about me. It's like I've been in counseling watching T.V."
- *Latrell Sprewell, explaining what he'd been doing during his NBA suspension for choking his coach*

"No. That stuff happens." *- Latrell Sprewell,*
1998, when asked if he was upset that his two pit bulls mauled his daughter

"Be good, or be gone." *- Bear Bryant*

"You're never too old until you think you are."
- Bear Bryant

"It's a lot better to be seen than heard. The sun is the most powerful thing I know of, and it doesn't make much noise." *- Bear Bryant*

"There are two types of preparation—physical and mental. You can't get by with just one or the other." *- Ken Stabler*

"Winning isn't imperative, but coming from behind and getting tougher in the fourth quarter is. I don't want you to think you have to win, because you don't. On the other hand, if you can go out there ripping and snorting and having fun by knocking people around, I assure you—you will win!"   - *Bear Bryant*

"At Alabama one morning at seven, I placed a call from my office to Shug Jordan or somebody at Auburn, and the girl said nobody was in yet. I said, 'Honey, what's wrong with you people over there? Don't y'all take football seriously?" - *Bear Bryant*

"Sure, I'd love to beat Notre Dame, don't get me wrong. But nothing matters more than beating that cow college on the other side of the state."
        - *Bear Bryant*

"First I prepare. Then I have faith." - *Joe Namath*

"I always want my players to show class—knock em' down, pat em' on the back and run back to the huddle." - *Paul Bryant*

"Mama wanted me to be a preacher. I told her coachin' and preachin' were a lot alike." - *Bear Bryant*

"I love football. I really love football. As far as I'm concerned, it's the second best thing in the world."
- *Joe Namath*

"There's nothing wrong with reading the game plan by the light of the jukebox." - *Ken Stabler*

"I can't wait for tomorrow. Why? Because I get better looking everyday." - *Joe Namath*

"**Never compromise what you think is right.**" - *Bear Bryant*

"**Never give up. Reach down inside and you'll find something left.**" - *Bear Bryant*

"**Mama told me to never wear a hat indoors.**"
   - *Bear Bryant when asked why he did not wear his houndstooth hat for the 1976 Sugar Bowl*

"**Never be too proud to get down on your knees and pray.**"
   - *Bear Bryant*

"Write home. I think everyone should find time to write and to go see their mother. I think that's healthy." - *Bear Bryant*

- 15 -

"I grew up pickin' cotton on my daddy's farm. To me, football is like a day off." - *Lee Roy Jordan*

"I guess I'm just too full of Bama." - *Tommy*
Lewis, explaining why he came off the sidelines to tackle Dickie Moegle in the 1954 Cotton Bowl, excerpted from The Wisdom of Southern Football *by Criswell Freeman*

"Offense sells tickets. Defense wins games." - *Bear Bryant*

"I just waxed the dude." - *Alabama defensive back Rory Turner's explanation of his game-saving tackle of Auburn's Brent Fullwood in the 17-15 1984 game*

"If you're ahead, play like you're behind. If you're behind, play like you're ahead." - *Bear Bryant*

"Have a plan in your life and be able to adjust it. Have a plan when you wake up, what you're going to do with your day. Just don't go lollygagging through any day in your life. I hope I have had some luck in my life because I have planned for the good times and the bad ones." - *Bear Bryant*

"I'm not as smart as other coaches. I have to work harder." - *Bear Bryant*

"Listen, does your boy know how to work? Try to teach him to work, to sacrifice, to fight. He'd better learn now, because he's going to have to do it someday." - *Bear Bryant*

"Bingo—That's a goodie!" - *Bear Bryant's popular expression for describing a fierce hit on his TV show*

"I don't really consider it a loss. We just ran out of
time." *- Bear Bryant, on losing to Notre Dame in the 1973 Sugar Bowl*

"Have a plan, not only for the day, but for the week and the
month and the year and ten years from now. Anticipate.
Plan. Anticipate every situation that could arise. Don't think
second by second what needs to be done. Have a plan.
Follow the plan, and you'll be surprised how successful you
can be. Most people don't plan. That's why it is easy to
beat most folks." *- Bear Bryant*

**"Never quit. It is the easiest cop-out in the world. Set a
goal and don't quit until you attain it. When you do
attain it, set another goal, and don't quit until you reach
it. Never quit."** *- Bear Bryant*

"A black newspaperman came up ad started talking smart, like he was looking for something. He said, 'How many black players you got on your team, Coach?' I said, 'I don't have any. I don't have any white ones, I don't have any black ones. I just have football players. They come in all colors.'" - *Bear Bryant*

"I tell my players they're special. They're something everybody should be proud of. They're not like the other students. I say, 'If you were we'd have fifteen thousand out for football.' You've got to take pride in being something special." - *Bear Bryant*

"There's a lot of blood, sweat, and guts between dreams and success." - *Bear Bryant*

"When folks are ignorant, you don't condemn them, you teach them." *- Paul Bryant*

"If anything goes bad, I did it. If anything goes semi-good, we did it. If anything goes really good, then you did it. That's all it takes to get people to win football games." *- Bear Bryant*

"I know this much: Alabama football will survive anything, because we play the most interesting football there is—we win."
- Bear Bryant

"Sports is the only place we have left where we can start even." *- Paul Bryant*

"First year, a .500 season. Second year, a conference championship. Third year, undefeated. Fourth year, a national championship. And by the fifth year, we'll be on probation, of course." - *Bear Bryant, Alabama football coach on his schedule for success at his alma mater*

"If you don't have anything but self-discipline, athletics is worthwhile." - *Bear Bryant*

"I can't imagine anyone who doesn't enjoy sex, who doesn't want sex all the time. It's the best thing ever invented." - *Joe Namath*

"Here's a twenty, bury two." - *Coach Bryant, after being asked to chip in ten dollars to help cover the cost of a sportswriters funeral*

"He's done more for integration in the South than Martin Luther King did in twenty years."

- University of Alabama assistant football coach Jerry Claiborne, on Sam Cunningham, an African-American back who led the University of Southern California to a 42-21 triumph over the Crimson Tide, an event that eventually led to Bear Bryant recruiting more black players

"If a coach doesn't have strong Alabama connections, then he doesn't belong in Alabama. I call this the *no yankees need apply* rule."

- Nancy Kincaid

"*Coach* is what you call him. It's a title, like *God*."

- Diane Roberts on University of Alabama football coach Gene Stallings

"One reason why we got what they call football preeminence here in the South is that we got a tradition of supervision and discipline. If I want a boy, I can put my hand on him in the dormitory. If he's just turned loose in town, no telling where he'll be."

-University of Alabama football coach, Gene Stallings

"The only president who's ever been fired at Alabama was against football. Any new president cuts his teeth on it, and better be for it. Because if he's not, they won't win, and if they don't win, he'll get fired."

- Bear Bryant

"Football is less a way out, than a way of life. No other sport has a chance in Alabama."

- Paul Hemphill

"Hold your horses, the elephants are coming."
- Writer Everett Strupper of the Atlanta Journal reported on a fan's exclamation as the eleven huge Alabama players rumbled on to the field

"It's kind of hard to rally 'round a math class."
- Bear Bryant on the role of athletics on the college campus

"It's the one where the player pitches the ball to the referee after a touchdown."
- Bear Bryant on his favorite play in football

"Football changes and so do people. The successful coach is the one who sets the trend, not the one who follows it."
- Bear Bryant

"Paul Bryant, the "great rehabilitator" at Maryland, Kentucky, and most recently at Texas A&M, now faces his stiffest challenge in 14 years as a head coach. He inherits an Alabama squad that has won only four of thirty games in the past three years."   *- Sports Illustrated, September 22, 1958.*

"The most serious invasion of the North since Lee was stopped at Gettysburg."   *- A Birmingham sportswriter in 1920, when two Southern college football squads were venturing North to contest "Yankee academies"*

"It's not the number of plays you have, it's how you execute them."   *- Bear Bryant*

"There ought to be a special place in heaven for coaches' wives."   *- Bear Bryant*

"He knocked me woozy. I have never been hit like that before and hopefully, I'll never be hit like that again." - *Steve Beuerlein, Notre Dame quarterback, after Cornelius Bennett's tackle of him in the 1986 game*

"Folks, this is the greatest individual defensive effort I have ever witnessed." - *CBS announcer Brent Musburger talking about Derek Thomas in the 1988 Penn State game*

"John Forney will always be the voice of the Crimson Tide. I may be the current custodian of the title, but he is the man that people always have and always will associate with that title." - *Eli Gold*

"I can't imagine being in the Hall of Fame with Coach Bryant. There ought to be two Hall of Fames, one for Coach Bryant and one for everybody else."
- Ozzie Newsome, upon his induction to the Alabama Hall of Fame

"In the second quarter, I saw Torretta (Gino) look over at me and he froze for a second. I saw fear."
- Bama defensive standout John Copeland

"If you don't have discipline, you can't have a successful program." *- Paul Bryant*

"If you believe in yourself and have dedication and pride--and never quit, you'll be a winner." *- Paul Bryant*

"I can reach a kid who doesn't have any ability as long as he doesn't know it." *- Paul Bryant*

"Sacrifice. Work. Self-discipline. I teach these things, and my boys don't forget them when they leave." *- Paul Bryant*

"Mama called." *- Coach Bryant's explanation for leaving a championship team at Texas A&M to return to his struggling alma mater*

"I don't hire anybody not brighter than I am. If they're not smarter than me, I don't need them." *- Bear Bryant*

"I'm known as a recruiter. Well, you've got to have chicken to make chicken salad." *- Bear Bryant*

"You must learn to hold a team together. You lift some men up, calm others down, until finally they've got one heartbeat. Then, you've got yourself a team." *- Bear Bryant*

"It's only a little bone." *- Coach Bryant after suiting up for the Crimson Tide against Arkansas in 1936, despite having a broken leg*

"Boys, I'd like to introduce you to Coach Wallace Wade. He's the man responsible for the great tradition of Alabama football."
- Bear Bryant, introducing Wade at a practice in 1980

"Tradition is a rich asset for any team. Tradition and success are traveling companions."   *- Wallace Wade*

"He (Bryant) always planned to win but he also taught you to have a plan if you lose. Now, I can relate to what he was saying better than when I was in school. All my days aren't winning national championships, and all my days aren't on top of the world. Life has its peaks, but it also has its valleys, and he (Bryant) was preparing us for those valleys, educating us on striving to win but also having a plan for when you don't win."
- Robby Rowan, former Alabama player under Bear Bryant

"The expectation level is high at the University of Alabama and it should be. What's wrong with people expecting excellence?"
- Former Alabama coach, Gene Stallings

"No, man, I majored in journalism. It was easier."
- Joe Namath responding to a reporter who asked him if he majored in basketweaving at Alabama, from Talk of the Tide

"I just want to thank God for blessing me with some athletic talent and letting me play for the University of Alabama."
- Derrick Thomas

"I've seen a lot of great college offensive linemen. The greatest was John Hannah." *- Bob Bell*

"Southern football is not recognized or respected. Boys, here's your chance to change that forever." - *Wallace Wade to the Alabama football team in 1926, just prior to the Tide's monumental, 20-19 Rose Bowl upset of a heavily-favored Washington team*

"The greatest southern football victory of all time was Alabama's Rose Bowl victory over Washington. It gained permanent esteem for southern football." - *George Leonard*

"Southerners regarded the rest of the nation with a complex mixture of assertive pride and defensive hostility, and intersectional football gave full rein to both of these sentiments. When Alabama defeated Washington, 20-19, in the 1926 Rose Bowl game, its display of masculine strength and virility . . . became proof that the martial prowess and chivalric grandeur of their mythologized ancestors [were] still alive in the modern world." - *Sports Historian Andrew Doyle, in the International Journal of Sport*

"Alabama, thy name is courage--unyielding valor in all its splendor! Flow on Crimson. Thou hast brought honors aplenty to Dixieland." *- Zipp Newman, January 1, 1927*

"Television exposure is so important to our program and so important to this university that we will schedule ourselves to fit the medium. I'll play at midnight, if that's what TV wants." *- Paul Bryant*

"There are a lot of nice stadiums we've played in. The loudest place I'd say would be Arkansas. But the most intimidating to me has got to be that ooooold place at LSU. The stadium is not even purple--it's a dull purple--a dull gold. But come game time, it's crazy. Coming to the stadium on game day--getting beers thrown at the bus. Every place you go you'll get a couple of guys making obscene gestures. But when people are actually shaking your bus--throwing beer. And I'm talking about close contact. Little kids--old men--everybody. Baton Rouge is the most intense."
    - Freddie Milons, Alabama receiver

"You learn you can do your best even when it's hard, even when you're tired and maybe hurting a little bit. It feels good to show some courage." *- Joe Namath*

"In Alabama, people won't say, 'My child was born in 1972.' They'll say, 'My child was born the year Auburn blocked two punts and beat Alabama.' That's how ingrained the sport is in our culture." *- Roy Kramer, SEC Commissioner*

"Nobody ever wins a football game — somebody loses it!" *- Wallace Wade, Alabama coach*

"He was the most impressive man I've ever been close to. When he walked into a room a hush came over it."
    - John Fornery, Alabama radio broadcaster, on Bear Bryant

"When he walked into a room, it was like his presence to there thirty seconds before he did. There was just something really special about him." - *Ron Franklin on Bear Bryant*

"Retire? Hell, I'd probably croak in a week!"
- Bear Bryant, who died in January, 1983, only 42 days after he retired as head coach of Alabama

"Don't talk too much or too soon." *- Bear Bryant*

"Even if you're not starting, you have to believe that you're as good as the guy who's playing in front of you. I've been second-string three times in my football career, and each time I thought I was better than the guy in front of me." *- Kenny "The Snake" Stabler*

"Proper conditioning is that fleeting moment between getting ready and going stale." - *Frank Thomas, Alabama football coach*

"You have to be willing to out-condition your opponents." - *Bear Bryant*

"It's the Alabama spirit—that indescribable something which made the efforts of a small team bring seemingly impossible results."
- *D.V. Graves*

"Alabama people sure love their football." - *Homer Smith*

"Be a gracious winner, and an understanding loser."
- *Joe Namath*

"When you win, there's glory enough for everybody. When you lose, there's glory for none." - *Bear Bryant*

"You play 50 or 60 plays a game for the privilege of making three or four that make the difference." - *Gene Stallings*

"When you win, nothing hurts." - *Joe Namath*

"Nobody wants to follow someone who doesn't know where he's going." - *Joe Namath*

"I don't have any ideas; my coaches have them. I just pass the ideas on and referee the arguments." - *Bear Bryant*

"One of the greatest things Coach Bryant used to do was pass along the credit." - *Gene Stallings*

"Growing up, we didn't have money or status. You had to work and hustle. Hustling made you resourceful and work made you hard, and I was doing both by the time I was eleven." - *Joe Namath*

"You never know how a horse will pull, until you hook him to a heavy load." - *Bear Bryant*

"Don't give up at halftime. Concentrate on winning the second half."
- *Bear Bryant*

"Football is an honest game. It's true to life. It's about sharing. Football is a team game. So is life." - *Joe Namath*

"Alabama fans love Bryant, and tolerate the rest of us."
- Gene Stallings

"The price of victory is high, but so are the rewards." *- Bear Bryant*

"Nobody ever got backslapped into winning anything."
- Wallace Wade

"All I know is that we went out there in two buses and we came back in one."
- Former Texas A&M player Gene Stallings, upon being asked if Coach Bryant's first practices at Texas A&M were as tough as reported

"Here's a moment you dream about happening, and here it was staring at us in the face. Gut-check time. Coach always preached it, jaw to jaw, cheek to cheek. They weren't going anywhere." *- Former Tide star Rich Wingo, of the goal-line stand in '79 for the National Championship*

"His ear had a real nasty cut and it was dangling from his head, bleeding badly. He grabbed his own ear and tried to yank it from his head. His teammates stopped him and the managers bandaged him. Man was that guy a tough one. He wanted to tear off his own ear so he could keep playing."
- Tennessee lineman Bull Bayer talking about his Alabama counterpart and first All-American Bully VandeGraaf in the 1913 game

"I was determined to block that field goal. There was no way I was going to let Alabama lose." *- Safety Stacy Harrison after blocking a field goal in the Tide's 9-6 win over Tennessee in 1990*

"Alabama's cornerbacks don't impress me one bit. They're overrated. Real men don't play zone defense and we'll show them a thing or two come January 1." *- Miami Receiver Lamar Thomas before the '93 Sugar Bowl, when he was involved in what many consider to be the play of the century in American college football*

"And believe me, to have been in the city of Tuscaloosa in October when you were young and full of Early Times and had a shining Alabama girl by your side--to have had all that and then to have seen those red shirts pour onto the field, and, then, coming behind them, with that inexorable big cat walk of his, the man himself, The Bear--that was very good indeed." - *Howell Raines, a Washington correspondent for the New York Times*

"Bryant can take his and beat yours, and then he can turn around and take yours and beat his."
- Houston Oiler head coach Bum Phillips, a former player under Coach Bryant

"If I could reach my students like that, I'd teach for nothing." *– An Alabama professor after seeing the players reaction to a pregame talk by Coach Bryant*

"Lee Roy was the best college linebacker - bar none. He would have made every tackle on every play if they had stayed in bounds." - *Coach Bryant on Lee Roy Jordan*

"You go by that and they'll have to fire us all."

- Former Auburn coach Shug Jordan on finding out that LSU coach Charlie McLendon had been fired for not being able to defeat Coach Bryant

"Sports is like war without the killing."

- Ted Turner

Arkansas

"You boys played like a wild band of Razorback hogs." - *Arkansas head football coach Hugo Bezdek, after he led his team to a 16-0 thrashing of Louisiana State University on October 30, 1909*

"It doesn't take a scientific rocket to find out what kind of offense we're going to run this year..." - *Danny Ford*

"Perhaps only in Arkansas will you see a deer crossing sign along a road ... at the airport! The University of Arkansas is literally in the middle of nowhere, but once inside the sparkling Bud Walton Arena it's like you're on Broadway. The building is dimly lit at the top of the arena and brilliantly illuminated at the bottom, which makes for a spotlight effect on the court. As soon as you enter, you know you're at an event. It's clearly theatre."
- *Glenn Guilbeau, The Baton Rouge Advocate, February 18, 2002*

"At Arkansas, they made a stamp to commemorate you; then, after last year, they had to stop making it because people were spitting on the wrong side."
- Lou Holtz, Arkansas coach

"A bird doesn't sing because it has an answer, it sings because it has a song."
- Lou Holtz

"I don't think we can win every game. Just the next one."
- Lou Holtz

"You never get ahead of someone as long as you try to get even with him."
—Lou Holtz

"When I look at all of you people in this room, I see no one look like me, talk like me or act like me...See, my great-great-grandfather came over on the ship, I didn't...And I don't think you understand what I'm saying. My great-great-grandfather came over on the ship. I did not come over on that ship, so I expect to be treated a little bit different. Because I know for a fact that I do not play on the same level as the other coaches around this school play on. I know that. You know it. And people of my color know that. And that angers me."

- Nolan Richardson

"It was about normal—no worse than an ordinary death march." *- Lou Holtz, on spring practice*

"They're used to being held all the time."

- Lou Holtz, on why big linemen are so secure

"If we win a game, I like for my players to be strong enough to carry me off of the field." - *Lou Holtz, on the importance of physical strength in his players*

"My athletes are always willing to accept my advice as long as it doesn't conflict with their views." - *Lou Holtz*

"My wife and I have a little trouble communicating. When I say 'broad,' she thinks about a trip to Europe. When she says 'diamond,' I think of baseball." - *Lou Holtz*

"A lifetime contract for a coach means if you're ahead in the third quarter and moving the ball, they can't fire you." - *Lou Holtz*

"It's a fine thing to have ability, but the ability to discover ability in others is the true test." - *Lou Holtz*

"I want to coach a team that opponents don't look forward to playing." - *Danny Ford*

"You must have dreams and goals if you are ever going to achieve anything in this world." - *Lou Holtz*

"You're never as good as everyone tells you when you win, and you're never as bad as they say when you lose." - *Lou Holtz*

"Life is ten percent what happens to you and ninety percent how you react to it." –*Lou Holtz*

"We have too many Marys and not enough Williams."
- *Lou Holtz, after taking over at William and Mary*

"Aerodynamically, the bumblebee is not supposed to fly. It's got a fat body and wings that are too small. But somebody forgot to tell the bumblebee." - *Nolan Richardson*

"I once busted my pants jumping up and down (at Arkansas). I was so animated, I split my pants. I always have an extra pair of pants in my locker, and this happened to be a home game, so that made it easier. I walked off the floor with coaches in front of me and behind me so no one could see." - *Nolan Richardson*

"Where did most of the slave ships stop? In the South." - *Nolan Richardson, Arkansas coach, 1998, on why there are so many good players in the SEC*

"I can say this, never had I had all these things happen in one day—Coach of the Year, the President comes to the game and hugs you and you win a trip to the Final Four." - *Nolan Richardson*

"If I were white, I'd be hailed as the next Jesus Christ." - *Nolan Richardson, after the 1994 National Championship*

"If they pay me the money, they can have their job tomorrow." - *Arkansas head basketball coach Nolan Richardson, under heavy criticism during a losing 2002 season*

"Basketball is my game. I love basketball and I live it and no matter how many points I score or how well I play, it still isn't enough."
- *John Adams, Arkansas basketball great*

"The President just blew my mind. It's not every day someone gets to meet and shake hands with the President. This is something that I can tell my grandkids."
- Corliss Williamson, after meeting Arkansas native Bill Clinton in 1994

"For the longest, football was the only thing we had going that we could really sink our resources into. Basketball at Arkansas was strong for many, many years until they kind of ran out of money and we had just enough money to have a football program. Basketball was still financially supported, but nothing the likes of what it should have been."
- Frank Broyles, Arkansas athletic director, on the early days

"I've found that God is usually on the side that has the best defensive tackles." *- Frank Broyles*

"The (1994) Championship gave Arkansas people something to rally around. People enjoy supporting and being involved in something like that because you have proven you can do something better than anybody else."

- Frank Broyles

"It was the most important significant rallying point of people in our state. Some of them had become lukewarm. The rabid fans were always there, but we joined forces with the lukewarm fans and those who had not even supported the Razorbacks, maybe in far corners of the state into a statewide mania." *- Frank Broyles, Arkansas athletic director on the 1994 National Championship*

"Eddie (Sutton) sat in my office and said, 'We've got to have a new facility,' I said, 'I promise you that we will get you a new facility.' That old theory of build it and they will come happened because he started winning his first year and the excitement took off and hadn't slowed down since." *- Frank Broyles, on the refurbishment of Barnhill Arena upon Eddie Sutton's arrival in 1974*

"My wife and my family are very pleased. They all forgot I had a good disposition." *- Frank Broyles, former Arkansas football coach, on leaving the profession*

"No, but you can see it from here." *- Lou Holtz, Arkansas football coach, when asked if Fayetteville was the end of the world*

"Some say God never sends you more than you can handle, but God may be overestimating my ability." *- Lou Holtz, Arkansas football coach*

"Sometimes the light at the end of the tunnel is a runaway train." *- Lou Holtz*

"Sure, I'd miss him, too." *- Frank Broyles, Arkansas athletic director, when asked if he would still like his football coach, Ken Hatfield, if his team went .500 this year*

"The first thing we look for in a house is its resale value." *- Beth Holtz, wife of Lou, when asked about her husband's peripatetic coaching career*

"Recruiting is and always will be an inexact and highly speculative science." *- Frank Broyles*

"No athletic program can ever be better than its recruiting."
- Frank Broyles

"My sales pitch to recruits was simple: At Arkansas, we have great fans, great traditions, and few distractions." *- Frank Broyles*

"When you go to a game in the South, you're likely to see four generations together. It's part of our heritage, and that heritage is passed along from generation to generation. It means something very important to our people." *- Frank Broyles*

"That's one of the biggest differences I've seen between football in the South and football anywhere else. On game day, the South has the most aggressive fans in America. In other parts of the country, fans are there to enjoy the game. But in the South, the fans believe they are there to participate!" - *Frank Broyles*

"Praise loudly. Criticize softly." - *Lou Holtz*

"Luck follows speed." - *Frank Broyles*

"They say a tie is like kissing your sister. I guess it's still better than kissing your brother."
- *Lou Holtz*

"You don't think about the close games you win—it's the close ones you lose that you think about."
- Frank Broyles

"When you lose, you doubt yourself and your plans. Losing creates doubt just like winning creates momentum."
- Danny Ford, Arkansas football coach

"Coaching is nothing more than eliminating mistakes before you get fired." *- Lou Holtz*

"Any athlete wants pride to compete against the best."
- Lance Alworth

"If you burn your neighbor's house down, it doesn't make your house look any better." *- Lou Holtz*

"The SEC gets dedicated football players. The ACC gets dedicated students."

*- Frank Howard, Clemson football coach, on the
difference between the two conferences*

Auburn

"If push comes to shove, I could lose all self-respect and become a reporter." *- Charles Barkley*

"It's hard to explain to others, but when Auburn and Georgia play it's like a game between you and your best friend." *- Vince Dooley, former Auburn graduate and Georgia Bulldog head football coach*

"Set your goals high, and don't stop till you get there."
- Bo Jackson

"When Auburn and Georgia play, it's like two brothers going at it in the backyard. I love my brother, but I want to whip him!"
- Pat Dye

"Coach "Shug" Jordan was a true gentleman, but he had a mean, cold streak to do what he had to do."
- Liston Eddings, Auburn defensive end

"If you're from Alabama you're either for the University of Alabama or you're for Auburn. You can't be both. And once you move here, you're asked to declare."
- Jim Fyffe, Auburn radio announcer

"My message is simple. Take control of your life."
- Charles Barkley

"I cut down to six meals a day."
- Charles Barkley, on losing weight

"I don't think there's any doubt. Anybody in their right mind know I'm the best forward in basketball. Well, the only person comparable to me is Karl Malone, but his body is so different from mine. Even my wife loves his body, and that's the main reason I say I'm the best. "With a body like that, he is supposed to be awesome. With a body like mine, I'm supposed to be a couch potato." — *Charles Barkley*

"They look like my daughter got a hold of some crayons and designed them." — *Charles Barkley, on the 76ers new uniforms*

"These guys who have three or four babies by different women should have their balls cut off."
— *Charles Barkley*

"We can't have a beer in the locker rooms. I can't have a beer after I run up and down the court for two hours, but they're going to serve it to the guy who's got a wife and two kids to drive home. That is so gutless. They're only concerned about making money."

- Charles Barkley

"New York is my kind of town, because I have a gun."
- Charles Barkley

"You can't even jump high enough to touch the rim unless they put a Big Mac on it." *- Charles Barkley to former Arkansas standout, Oliver Miller*

"The secret of Auburn's success? The fans. The Auburn people are the secret greatness of Auburn." *- Pat Dye*

"I don't know if that's a great team, but they most certainly were great against us. I don't guess anybody has ever hit us that hard."
- Auburn coach Shug Jordan, 1961

"A coach simply must resign himself to the fact that he is no longer involved with the educational process, but with entertainment." *- Ralph "Shug" Jordan, Auburn football coach*

"Where crouching tigers wait their hapless prey... Sweet Auburn, loveliest village of the plain..."
- Oliver Goldsmith, excerpted from his poem, "The Deserted Village," published in 1770

"There will never be another player like me. I'm the ninth wonder of the world." *- Charles Barkley, on himself*

"Pressure is for tires." *- Barkley on pressure*

"I know that I'm never as good or bad as any single performance. I've never believed my critics or my worshippers, and I've always been able to leave the game at the arena."   *- Charles Barkley*

"I decided to come back to Auburn and finish my degree because there is something magical about the orange and blue. I don't think I could graduate from any other university."   *- Chuck Person*

"It means people will be able to see that I don't have the biggest butt in the league." *- Charles Barkley, 250 pound NBA forward, on the advantages of playing alongside newly-acquired 255 pound Rick Mahorn*

"That's going to happen anytime you write a book, so I just have to deal with the heat."

> *- Charles Barkley, 1992, when he tried to block the publication of his own autobiography, "Outrageous," because he had been "misquoted" in his own book; from the book "They Said That!" by Larry Engelman*

"Japan makes the best cars, Italians make the best clothes, why can't we be the best at something too?"

> *- Charles Barkley, 1992, explaining what's right about the Dream Team, the American basketball team in the Olympic Games*

"I'm quitting this team for the swim team. I'm going to the pool as long as there are babes with no tops. You'll think I'm Mark Spitz before this week is over."

> *- Charles Barkley, 1992, at the Olympic Games in Barcelona, after hearing that Monaco's women's swim team practices topless*

"It was like I was president. No not our President, sorry. A *real* president." *- Charles Barkley, 1992, on being a star in the Olympic Games (Bill Clinton was in office at the time)*

"I miss America. I miss crime and murder. There hasn't been a brutal stabbing or anything here the last 24 hours. I've missed it." *- Charles Barkley, 1992, after the American Dream Team beat Lithuania by 51 points in the Olympics*

"You can't compare preseason to regular season. Preseason is just a way to screw fans out of money." *- Charles Barkley, 1992*

"I can be bought. If they paid me enough money, I'd work for the Ku Klux Klan." *- Charles Barkley, 1992, when asked if he'd ever play again for the 76ers*

"I hear Tonya Harding is calling herself the Charles Barkley of figure skating. I was going to sue her for defamation of character, but then I realized, I have no character." - *Charles Barkley, 1994*

"There wouldn't be any such thing as Death Row, there'd be Death Week. If you killed someone in a violent way, you would be dead within a week." - *Charles Barkley, 1994, on his position on violent crime and drugs if he held public office*

"The players today…they're like what you see on T.V. Kids killing kids and stuff like that. Kids in gangs. I think that's the generation of the young player coming to the NBA. Rebellious. Undisciplined. They speak for our society. I mean, if they didn't play basketball, theyd be the guys who'd be in gangs, who'd kill somebody." - *Charles Barkley, 1994*

"The majority of poor people and minorities vote Democratic. 1
why they're poor and their options are limited." *- Charles Barkley*

"When I talk trash, I'm just having fun with it. I'm not trying to embarrass a guy. I don't say, "I'm going to kill you. Larry, Magic and Michael—these guys talked trash, but it was a friendly kind of trash. We didn't cuss other players out. Every time we scored on a guy, we didn't get in his face and stare at him. I think that' just wrong."
- Charles Barkley, 1994

"Grandma, I am rich!" *- Charles Barkley, on his response to his grandmother's complaint that Republicans are only for the rich*

"The NBA's in disarray—a white guy won the slam-dunk competition. We need to have another Million Man March."
- Charles Barkley, 1996, on teammate Michael Finley's loss to L.A. Clippers rookie Brent Barry

"I told you white boys you've never heard of a '90s nigger. We do what we want to do. I'm going to be a little more vocal now..."
- Charles Barkley, 1992, unhappy with playing with the 76ers

"If I weren't earning $3 million a year to dunk a basketball, most people on the street would run in the other direction if they saw me coming." - *Charles Barkley*

"I don't believe professional athletes should be role models. I believe parents should be role models...It's not like it was when I was growing up. My mom and my grandmother told me how it was going to be. If I didn't like it, they said, 'Don't let the door hit you on the ass on your way out.' Parents have to take better control." - *Charles Barkley*

"These are my new shoes. They're good shoes. They won't make you rich like me, they won't make you rebound like me, they definitely won't make you handsome like me. They'll only make you have shoes like me. That's it." *- Charles Barkley*

"Every kid I talk to thinks they're going to be in the NBA. I gotta be honest with you. You're not going to be." *- Charles Barkley*

I know that I a not a Democrat, because I don't think Democrats have done a good job helping black people or poor people...I guess the only thing left for me is to be a Republican." *- Charles Barkley*

"I think we should play all 3 of those teams and get the hell out of town." - *Charles Barkley, 1996, after the Dream Team was forced to evacuate their hotel room due to a bomb threat*

"People are complaining that I'm working 40 minutes three days a week?" What a great country." - *Charles Barkley, on worries that he is courting injury by playing too many minutes*

"Heck no. A guy threw a drink on me, and I threw him through a window. I was just mad and I was on a higher floor." - *Charles Barkley, 1988, when asked if the reason he quit drinking was a recently publicized altercation with a man in a ground-level bar*

"I got the superstar treatment. Everybody else got bologna and water. I got bologna and milk." - *Charles Barkley, on the four hours he once spent in a Milwaukee jail*

"Philadelphia is somewhat of a racist city...Let's not kid ourselves. There are just as many black racists as there are white racists...People never say I'm wrong. They just say I shouldn't say it." - *Charles Barkley*

"Pat is the most complete quarterback I've ever seen. When he's in the game there's not one thing your offense is not capable of doing." - *Shug Jordan*

"He does more things to beat you than any other quarterback I've seen." - *Bear Bryant on Pat Sullivan*

"You know it's all going to hell when the best rapper out there is white and the best golfer is black." - *Charles Barkley*

"It takes the dignity out of college athletics when you have a guy playing football who can't spell football." - *Bo Jackson*

"My mind is always going, always spinning. I try to think of something to be the next Bill Gates." - *Bo Jackson*

"I got all that out of my system before I got married. Now, every town I go to, women come chasing after me, calling my room, sending me notes, but I don't pay them any attention. I wouldn't want any woman who chases after me, and I stopped chasing after them once I taught my wife how to fire my pistol." - *Bo Jackson*

"When in doubt, punt!" - *John Heisman*

"I used to be a Chippendale. Now I'm a Clydesdale."
- Charles Barkley, on aging

"Hal Baird is a great coach–an excellent pitching coach.
While I was there I learned a lot of things that helped move
me on to the next level. Playing at Auburn for three years
was my equivalent of playing three years in the minor
leagues. I received that kind of experience and teaching
while I was at Auburn."
- Gregg Olson, relief pitcher, Kansas City Royals, Auburn Tiger (1986-88)

"Coach Baird is a professor of the game. He taught me a
great deal while I was at Auburn and took my baseball skills
to another level." *- Frank Thomas, first baseman, Chicago White Sox,
Auburn Tiger (1987-89)*

"Always remember that Goliath was a 40 point favorite over little David." - *Ralph "Shug" Jordan*

"There's a closeness that all Auburn people feel. It's the war eagle spirit." - *Shug Jordan*

"When we play Alabama, the coaches don't need to prepare pep talks." - *Shug Jordan*

"Men, there is a time for everything. A time to live and a time to die; a time to love and a time to hate; a time for peace and a time for war; And gentleman, there's a time to beat Alabama. That time is now!"
   - Shug Jordan, prior to the 1969 Alabama-Auburn contest

"All I ask is that you give everything you've got on every play. That's not asking very much." - *Shug Jordan*

"Tucker Frederickson was the most complete football player I've seen in the 40 years I've been connected with the game." - *Shug Jordan*

"Gentlemen, it is better to have died as a small boy than to fumble this football." - *John Heisman*

"Don't cuss. Don't argue with the officials. And don't lose the game..." - *John Heisman*

"When you find your opponent's weak spot, **hammer it!**" - *John Heisman*

"When people tell me I could be the best athlete there is, I just let it go in one ear and out the other. There is always somebody out there who is better than you are. Go ask Mike Tyson." *- Bo Jackson*

"We went undefeated last year. It's going to be awful difficult to improve on our record." *– Shug Jordan, August 1958*

"At Auburn, practice is hell. But when you line up across from the big, fast, smart, angry boys from florida, and Georgia, and Alabama, where there is no quality of mercy on the ground and no place to hide, you'll know why practice is hell at Auburn." *- Pat Dye*

"If you're a football coach, criticism comes with the territory. If it tears you up, you better get into another profession." *- Pat Dye*

"Baseball and football are very different games. In a way, both of them are easy. Football is easy if you're crazy as hell. Baseball is easy if you've got patience. They'd both be easier for me if I were a little more crazy-and a little more patient." - *Bo Jackson*

"If my mother put on a helmet and shoulder pads and a uniform that wasn't the same as the one I was wearing, I'd run over her if she was in my way. And I love my mother." - *Bo Jackson*

"It is better to give a lick than receive one. If anybody got in my way, I tried to run right through them."
                                                      - *Bo Jackson*

"I was born and raised on a farm and when you watch those crops grow, you learn to be patient." - *Pat Dye*

"This (Alabama) is the number one football state in America…people in Wyoming are talking rodeo in July. The people in Alabama are talking the Alabama-Auburn football game. The people in North Carolina are talking the four corners offense. In Alabama, they're talking about why you didn't run the ball on third down and one instead of throwing it." - *Pat Dye*

"Don't wait to be a great man. Be a great boy."
- Paul Grist, Shug Jordan's first coach, a phrase Jordan repeated regularly to his players

"We're going to Atlanta with only one thing in mind…to beat the hell out of Georgia Tech!" - *Shug Jordan*

"We weren't sure of anything when Coach Dye came in. But we did know that we were going to have to work. He said that spring practice would be like going through a briar patch in a storm. He said it was going to be tough and he didn't give us any false ideas."

- Greg Carr, from David Housel's book, From the Desk of David Housel

"I struck out with two men on base. I was so angry, so frustrated, I turned and without even thinking about it, snapped my bat over my thigh. The bat split right in half. Afterward, reporters asked me if it was the first time I'd ever broken a bat over my thigh. I said, 'I broke an aluminum bat over my knee in college.' I was just kidding." *- Bo Jackson*

"I thought the second plane was going to pour water on the building. But it didn't."

- Auburn coach Tommy Tuberville on watching the terrorist attacks that toppled the World Trade Center September 11, 2001

"Be careful of that team from Cumberland. There's no telling what they have up their sleeves."

- John Heisman, Georgia Tech coach, with his team ahead by the score of 136-0, at halftime of Tech's infamous 222-0 victory over Cumberland College

"After years of bondage, our people were finally delivered to the Promised Land."

- David Housel, Auburn athletics director, after Auburn defeated a #2 ranked Alabama team by the score of 30-20—the first time the game had been played in Auburn

"What I remember most is that time after time we had him, but he always found a way to make the play."

- Vince Dooley on Auburn quarterback Pat Sullivan

"If you're lucky, you get to coach one like him in a lifetime, and I was lucky."

- Pat Dye, on coaching Bo Jackson at Auburn

"Don't run too fast through life. You only have one." *- Bo Jackson*

"Life is short. Don't waste any of it carrying around a load of bitterness. It only sours your life, and the world won't pay any attention anyway." *- Pat Dye*

"Today, not tomorrow." *- Terry Bowden, Auburn head football coach*

"You can never tell when a break is coming your way. That's why you've got to go all out on every play." *- Shug Jordan*

"Always remember that Goliath was a 40-point favorite over Little David." *- Shug Jordan*

"I don't believe in miracles. I believe in character." *- Pat Dye*

"Have a profound respect for discipline." *- Shug Jordan*

"You're the only person who can decide where you want to go and how you're going to get there."
- Terry Bowden

"Nothing has changed about what makes a winner. A winner works his butt off and is dependable. He's not always the most talented, but he gives everything on every play." - *Pat Dye*

"The true football fan pays no attention to time or mileage when there is a big game to see." - *John Heisman*

"I don't believe in a jinx or a hex. Winning depends on how well you block and tackle." - *Shug Jordan*

"Coaches should be masterful, commanding, even dictatorial. A coach has no time to say 'please' or 'mister.' Occasionally he must be severe." - *John Heisman*

"Football is not an 'I' game, it's a 'we' game."

- Pat Dye

"Athletes make men strong, study makes men wise and character makes men great." *- Cliff Hare*

"Thrust your projections into their cavities, grasping them about the knees and depriving them of their means of propulsion. They must come to earth, locomotion being denied them." *- John Heisman, on how to tackle*

"WE MAY NOT BE THE BEST FOOTBALL TEAM IN AMERICA, BUT THERE IS NO REASON WE CAN'T BE THE BEST CONDITIONED TEAM." *- Pat Dye, from David Housel's book, From the Desk of David Housel*

"...a prolate spheroid—that is, an elongated sphere—on which the outer leathern casing is drawn tightly over a somewhat small rubber tubing." - *John Heisman*

"Successful coaches are few and far between. It's a wonder they command salaries without limit."
- *John Heisman*

"...there are few instances of alleged entertainment and relaxation that can match a college football game in stirring the deepest flames of partisanship and outright provincialism. And down South you can color that partisanship passionate!"

- Keith Jackson

Florida

"Call me arrogant, cocky, crybaby, whiner or whatever names you like. At least they're not calling us losers anymore." - *Steve Spurrier*

"Blindfolded with his back to the wall, with his hands tied behind him, Steve Spurrier would still be a two-point favorite at his own execution." - *The Atlanta Journal Constitution on the "Evil Genius," from Bragging Rights by Richard Ernsberger*

"I may win and I may lose, but I will never be defeated." - *Emmitt Smith*

"The loudest, most obnoxious and notorious piece of real estate in all of college football."
                    - *The Atlanta Journal Constitution on "The Swamp"*

"Throwing the football is fun. We try to keep a balance in between running and throwing, but we're different from most other teams. We pass to set up the run; most everyone else does it the other way around. It works for us, and until we see that it won't work, we'll keep doing it. We try to throw the ball on a timing basis. It doesn't always work out that way, but our routes are precise, exact, and sharp. The ball should get to you the moment you're creating space between you and the defender." *- Dwayne Dixon, receivers coach under*
Steve Spurrier

"The swamp is where the Gators live. We feel comfortable there, but we hope our opponents feel tentative. A swamp is hot and sticky and dangerous." *- Steve Spurrier*

"He's got a peculiar side. Most coaches get hung up on the opposition. He's only concerned about his offense."
- Paul Finebaum, on Steve Spurrier

"I can't wait to get back to the restaurant and see the waiter who said, 'Cheerios and Notre Dame are different: Cheerios belong in a bowl.'"
- Lou Holtz, after Notre Dame upset Florida in the 1992 Sugar Bowl

"That's the good thing about coaching, when you can develop a relationship with players who relate to you as a person, as a counselor and a brother. You've got to be there for them and help motivate them and keep them on track. You can't save them all. Those that will listen to you are the ones you want to go out and prosper."
- Dwayne Dixon

"What does it take to be the best? Everything. And everything is up to you." *- Emmitt Smith*

"Coach Lopez told me that you can come and play for a national title or watch us play for a national title. Now that we're in Omaha, he is a man of his word."
- Paul Rigdon, 1996

"That's the great thing about baseball. You don't have the great athletes like you do in football or basketball. You have to get the players to believe. Andy has his players believing." *- Skip Bertman, LSU head coach on Andy Lopez*

"Andy Lopez has been in knife fights, he's been shot at, punched, kicked in the face...and survived the mean streets of Rancho San Pedro, L.A. A quarter of a century later, the baseball coach at the University of Florida still talks tough, walks with a bit of a swagger, watches his back, and yes, he remains the great persuader."
- Mike Bianchi, Florida Times Union

"We just try to go out there and play the game and just play against the game, like Coach Lopez says. We don't play against a certain team. We play against the game, as Coach says, and the game will come to you." — *Brad Wilkerson in 1996*

"The crowd tonight was the best crowd we faced since I've been the Kentucky coach."

- Rick Pitino, Kentucky head coach, afterFlorida's 79-62 home victory over the 10th-ranked Wildcats

"I want my players to think as positively as the 85-year old man who married a 25-year old woman and bought a five-bedroom house next to the elementary school."

- Charley Pell, Florida football coach

"Apparently you've never been here. You *will* be impressed.
Your ears will ring for days. There is something to be said
when it's 100 degrees outside—and yet when the team runs
through the tunnel you get chill bumps. There is something to
be said about that."

- A Florida fan to Richard Ernsberger in his book, Bragging Rights

"In the SEC, every Saturday game is like the Super Bowl." *- Jessie Palmer*

"You tell Coach Fulmer that the Swamp is going to be loud this year. As loud as its ever been." *- Steve Spurrier, to Richard Ernsberger, author of Bragging Rights*

"Discover the talent that God has given you. Then, go out and make the most of it."

- Steve Spurrier

"But the real tragedy was that 15 hadn't been colored yet." *- Steve Spurrier, Head Coach of the Florida Gators, in 1991, telling fans that a fire at Auburn's football dorm had destroyed 20 books*

"If I'm a good football coach, it's because of my mistakes. I try to learn from them." *- Steve Spurrier*

"We said before the game that this was going to be a fifteen round heavyweight fight." *- Jon Hoke, Florida defensive coordinator*

"Two-bits, four-bits, six-bits, a dollar...all for the Gators get up and holler!" - *George Edmundson, Florida's "Mr. Two Bits"*

"A lot of people say it tastes like chicken. But I say it tastes like gator." - *Jeanne Britton of Hawthorne, Florida, who sells genuine gator heads on University Ave. in Gainesville*

"Only gators can survive a trip to the Swamp." - *Steve Spurrier*

"We didn't do much today except throw to the air, and the air was tough on us. Better today than Saturday, right Mick?"
- *Steve Spurrier, to Mike Hubert, Florida radio announcer*

"Yeah, be quiet when we have the ball, please. We gotta do some [play] checking and some signals, and we need to hear. But be as loud as you want when they got the ball. But try to be quiet when the Gators have it." *- Steve Spurrier, to Florida fans prior to the Tennessee game at home in the Swamp*

"I've dated girls who were far better looking than the quality of the girls who would be going out with me." *- Chris Collinsworth, on the advantages of playing pro football*

"Danny Wuerffel is a better person than he is a quarterback, and he is a great, great quarterback." *- Steve Spurrier*

"I enjoy football, but it has never been the most important thing in my life." *- Danny Wuerffel, 1996*

"I've got a friend whose body temperature goes up three degrees on game weekends, he gets so worked up." - *Bruce "The Lizard Man" Doyle, Gainesville house painter, from Bragging Rights*

"Florida has its own North and South, but its northern area is strictly Southern, and its southern area is strictly Northern." - *Florida, A Guide to the Southernmost state*

"If people like you too much, it's probably because they're beating you." - *Steve Spurrier*

"Mississippi State was No. 1 in pass defense coming in. They won't be going out." - *Steve Spurrier, after his Gators threw for 507 yards in a 52-0 stomping of the Bulldogs in 2001*

"I'm announcing my retirement today Jan. 4, 2002, as head football coach at the University of Florida. I simply believe that 12 years as head coach at a major university in the SEC is long enough. I thank all the players, assistant coaches, support staff people and the greatest football fans in the world for the success we have shared the last 12 years. I also personally thank all the Gators that went to the Orange Bowl to support our team last Wednesday night in my final game. I believe Jeremy Foley, who has a reputation of hiring outstanding coaches, will bring a coach to Florida that will do just as well or better in the years to come. I believe I'm certainly not the only coach to be able to win consistently at Florida. Our football program is in excellent shape and the next coach will inherit a very talented team, just like I did from Galen Hall's program in 1990. I've had a wonderful working relationship with all my bosses over the past 12 years. I thank Bob Bryan for hiring me, and I thank

Bill Arnsparger, Jeremy Foley, President John Lombardi and President Chuck Young for allowing me to run the football program. I'm not burned out, stressed out or mentally fatigued from coaching. I just feel my career as a college head coach after 15 years is complete and if the opportunity and challenge of coaching a NFL team happens it is something I would like to pursue. I believe that the University of Florida is the best place for a high school football player to get an education and play football in the best stadium, 'The Swamp,' before the best football fans in the world. Again, I thank the `Gator Nation' for the overwhelming support of our teams for 12 years. The seven SEC championships and the 1996 national championship are memories of a lifetime that we will all share together. I'm a Gator and will be for the rest of my life."

- Stephen Orr Spurrier's resignation speech, January 4, 2002

"Football is a religion in the Southland, played by boys and relived daily by their families."

- *Zipp Newman*

Georgia

"If the world was ending tomorrow, your one wish should be that we are playing Auburn today."
- Steve Sleek, Georgia Bulldog lineman

"What's important isn't what folks say about you, but how you feel about yourself." *- Herschel Walker*

"Football is important in the SEC, and the standards are high. We can be ranked 14th in the nation and still be ranked 3rd in the SEC Eastern Division. It's a tough conference."
- Vince Dooley, Georgia athletic director

"He'd better go to Georgia."

- Herschel Walker on where his son might play college football, if he had the chance, from Georgia Bulldog Magazine, September, 2000

"I've done well in football, and now I want to do well in life. I love the University of Georgia and the state of Georgia. When I was at Georgia Sanford Stadium wasn't as big as it is now, but we had a real down-home atmosphere there, and that's what was important. If you have your family around you, you're O.K. And the University of Georgia has always been like family to me."

- Herschel Walker, 2000

"Snap. Over his head and out of the endzone for a safety! They've given us two points! Can you believe that? They snapped that ball a hundred miles in a tight spiral and blew it over the punter's head in the back of the endzone and in the hedge—the wounded hedge. Safety!" *- Larry Munson, "The Voice of the Georgia Bulldogs," calling a play that gave Georgia a 15-14 lead over the Ole Miss Rebels*

"It was a little different. It was like playing inside."
- Steve Webber, 1990 World Series Champion Georgia Bulldog baseball coach, after his team played a game inside the Louisiana Superdome

"I thought he would be great, but I didn't think he'd be that great that soon." - *Vince Dooley, Georgia Football Coach, on the greatness of Herschel Walker*

"Happiness is being able to lay your head on the pillow at night and sleep." - *Herschel Walker*

"I shouldn't get the credit for all those records at Georgia. I had an extremely good offensive line for three years. A lot of these long runs I had were due to excellent blocking."
- *Herschel Walker*

"Coach Dooley is the key to my success today. He disciplined me just as my mother and father did, which was very important. He made me realize that unless I worked hard, I was no one special."

- Herschel Walker

"Leadership must be demonstrated, not announced." *- Fran Tarkenton, Georgia Bulldog*

"The definition of an atheist in Alabama is a person who doesn't believe in Bear Bryant." *- Wally Butts, Georgia football coach*

"Beware the big plays. The eighty yard drive is better than the eighty yard pass." *- Fran Tarkenton*

"When you talk about playing as a team, that was the team. It was unbelievable. I don't know that any team ever played better together than that one. Coach Dooley and the seniors on that team made us believe in each other. We didn't beat people because we were more talented, we beat people because we played together. We won as a team." *- Herschel Walker*

"It's a lonesome walk to the sidelines, especially when thousands of people are cheering your replacement." - *Fran Tarkenton*

"To err is human, to forgive is divine. But to forgive a football coach is unheard of." *- Vince Dooley*

"As a coach, the alumni you have to worry about is the ones you never see." *- Wally Butts*

"Herschel had world-class speed and strength. I've seen others who had both of those, but he also had mental toughness and self-discipline. I've never seen another back combine those qualities like he did."

- Vince Dooley, on Herschel

"It's not how good you are when you play good. It's how good you are when you play bad. And we played pretty good, even though we played bad. Imagine if we'd played good." *- Litterial Green, Georgia guard, after the Bulldogs defeated Georgia Tech 66-65*

"I don't care where a man comes from or how he spells his name. All I ask is that he be loyal to Georgia, proud of that jersey and try like the devil to win."

- Vince Dooley

"The cost of bats doesn't affect the big schools like it does the small ones, because of the bat contracts enjoyed by schools in larger conferences. However, the goal is to make the new bats heavier, and in that regard more like the wooden bats--a wooden bat that doesn't break, if you will."

- Ron Polk, Georgia Bulldog head baseball coach

"Keep rules to a minimum and enforce the ones you have."

- Vince Dooley

"There are two kinds of discipline: self-discipline and team discipline. You need both." *- Vince Dooley*

"You've got to do everything well, but you've got to play defense first." *- Vince Dooley*

"I never get tired of running. The ball ain't that heavy."
- Herschel Walker

"Go you silver britches!" *- Georgia fan cheer*

"Atlanta will be the scene Saturday of the first interstate intercollegiate football game (Georgia vs. Auburn); both teams have been practicing for weeks." *- Atlanta Journal, February 17, 1892*

"How 'bout them Dogs!" *– Georgia fan cheer, 1980*

"He was a coach's dream because of his attitude, not only in what he said but what he did. He was a total team player despite the incredible individual skills he had."

- Vince Dooley, on Herschel Walker

"Tradition is defined as the handing down of beliefs, legends, and customs from generation to generation."
- University of Georgia football media guide

"Uga is the best mascot a team could have. He'll lay on you. He'll lick on you. Give him a bone and he'll love you for life."
- Clarence Kay, former Georgia and Denver Bronco receiver

"The Cowboys got nothing more than a handful of Minnesota smoke." *- Randy Galloway, sportswriter, opining on the trade of Herschel Walker to the Minnesota Vikings for eight players, many of whom went on to help Dallas win 3 Super Bowls*

"If you train hard, you'll not only be hard, you'll be hard to beat." *- Herschel Walker*

''Uga's injury has gotten more national attention than my two running backs (Tim Worley and Keith Henderson, who both had serious injuries in 1986).'' *- Vince Dooley complaining after learning that Uga IV would undergo knee surgery*

"My God, we've just beaten Tennessee in Knoxville!"
- Larry Munson, Voice of the Bulldogs, after Georgia came from behind to defeat Tennessee 35-31, in 1973

"I didn't just hear from Georgia people, but from people from all over the South. To go up there and invade the North and come back a winner was the greatest thing for a lot of people. It was as if we had had a chance to go to Gettysburg again." *- Vince Dooley, on the reaction from the fans after his Bulldogs defeated Michigan in Ann Arbor in 1965*

"I really didn't understand what was going on in that stadium, but I knew that when those people came back, they were either very happy or very sad. I figured it must be pretty important." *- Bill Curry, former Georgia Tech player, and Alabama and Kentucky coach, describing what it was like growing up in Athens in the backyard of the University of Georgia*

"Between the hedges." *- Grantland Rice, legendary sportswriter, credited with coining the popular term used to describe Georgia's advantaged setting over its opponents at Sanford Stadium*

"If you haven't done the preparation on Monday through Friday, there's nothing magical you can do on Saturday to get your team ready to play the game. Teams are most confident when they know they are prepared." *- Vince Dooley*

"As soon as the last bowl game is over in January, most of the people I know start counting the days until the next season gets here. A lot of us live and die by the kick off in the fall. A lot of friendships are built and maintained for a lifetime thanks to college football."

- Bandon "Booger" Seely, longtime Albany, Georgia Bulldog fan

"In the South, college football bears the imprint of the Civil War—taking territory and committing acts of controlled violence for what coaches tell the boys is honor."

- Diane Roberts

Kentucky

"Teamwork is the essence of life." *- Pat Riley, former Rupp Runt*

"Potential is a French word that means you aren't worth a damn yet." *- Jeff Van Note*

"There's no such thing as coulda, shoulda and woulda. If you shoulda and coulda, you woulda done it." *- Pat Riley*

"Both teams used basically the same offense, which is based on having the ball." - Fran Curci, Kentucky football coach, in his weekly UK football newsletter

"Even today, the character of great tradition permeates the Memorial Coliseum air with near spiritual force."
- University of Kentucky Basketball Media Guide

"True motivation is not getting people to play their potential. True motivating is getting people to play beyond their potential." *- Rick Pitino*

"In the storied land of Kentucky Colonels, there dwelled but one Baron, a man of consummate pride and a molder of powerful teams which for more than four decades made the name University of Kentucky synonymous with the game of basketball."
- University of Kentucky Media Guide on Coach Adolph Rupp

"I want them to use the court to express themselves. But on the other hand, I don't want them to be flip. I don't want to be good old Riley to the players, the guy they could treat as an old shoe."
- Pat Riley, professional coach

"Every time your back is against the wall, there is only one person that can help you. And that's you. It comes from the inside." - *Pat Riley*

"In the next four or five years, Kentucky will be at its best. It has taken a lot of hard labor, but down the road we will be at our best." - *Rick Pitino, 1995*

"You can make mistakes and be forgiven, but dishonesty lingers in people's memories forever. It's much easier to keep your reputation than rebuild it. Lying makes a problem part of your future; truth makes a problem part of your past." - *Rick Pitino*

"Tubby Smith has carried on the unbelievable traditions of Wildcat basketball—a first-class program in every way. Kentucky basketball stands for greatness year-in and year-out. It's awesome baby, with a capital 'A.'" *- Dick Vitale, National Broadcast Analyst*

"If something had happened to that ball, we couldn't have played." *- Thomas G. Bryant, member of the original Kentucky basketball team in 1903, when a group of students collectively chipped in three dollars to purchase a ball*

"Those boys certainly are not concert violinists, but they sure can fiddle!" *- Adolph Rupp describing his fourth national championship team, the "Fiddlin' Five," after their defeat of Seattle, 84-72*

"Really, UCLA's a great place as well, but they don't have the kind of environment they have here. The fans here have a passion." *- Dick Vitale on Kentucky fans, December 23, 1999*

"Apparently the University of Kentucky basketball dynasty is to continue forever."

- Philadelphia Inquirer, December 23 1954

"Turner ... Burner .... and one" *- Jim Nantz*

"Kentucky has found the secret of basketball, that it's five guys playing together."

- Former University North Carolina coach Frank McGuire

"You have no choice about how you lose, but you do have a choice about how you come back and prepare to win again." - *Pat Riley*

"I'd just as soon freeze to death."

- Actress Ashley Judd relating a story of being offered a University North Carolina Chapel Hill jacket on a chilly movie set, Lexington Herald Leader, August 15, 1996

"It's not wise to come to Kentucky and try to run them off their court. Not too many teams have ever done that."
- *Mississippi State Coach Babe McCarthy in 1962*

"When you see Kentucky's fans, you just wonder. You think how wonderful it would be to go to their school. You wish you could trade places for a day, just so you could experience that feeling." - *UCLA player Kris Johnson*

"They had it before you, they had it during you, they'll have it when you're gone..."   - *Al McGuire on Kentucky Basketball Tradition*

"I don't want to be part of an organization that does not have high expectations." - *Pat Riley*

"I have to believe it was all in the hair."   - *Actor and producer Michael Douglas, to Pat Riley, referring to his hair style that Douglas copied for his Academy-Award winning performance in Wall Street*

"This will be the first time the referee drops the ball."
- *Former Kentucky great Dan Issel, announcing for the Denver Nuggets, anticipating a jump ball between Denver's 5'10" Michael Adams and Charlotte's 5'3" Mugsy Bogues*

"That's our mother-in-law set—constant nagging and harassment."
- Rick Pitino, Kentucky head basketball coach, when asked about one of the Wildcat's defensive alignments

"TWC . . . TWC? What's that stand for, Two White Coaches?" - *Adolph Rupp, after hearing of the controversial decision by Texas Western's coach Don "The Bear" Haskins to start an all-black lineup in the 1966 National Championship game*

"All I want out of life is to get a bunch of boys together and whip somebody else." - *Adolph Rupp*

"Boys, when you go home tonight, I want you to look long and hard at these rankings. One. Two. Three. Kentucky, Duke, Vanderbilt. All from the South. And all white. Read it and remember. You'll never see it happen again."
- *Adolph Rupp to his players during the 1965-66 basketball season*

"At least we're still the Number One white team in the country." *- Lexington Herald-Leader sports editor Billy Thompson, addressing the annual Kentucky Athletic Department Banquet a week after Texas Western had claimed the national championship from Adolph Rupp's "Runts"*

"This team ain't worth a damn, but it just doesn't know it." *- Adolph Rupp, Kentucky basketball coach*

"I know there have been a lot of people who thought he was a racist. But I think the times can dictate how people act -- where you're brought up, how you're brought up. If he was a racist, he wasn't alone in this country. I'm never going to judge anybody.... That's a long time ago, too ... You learn from the past, and you go on." *- Tubby Smith, Kentucky head basketball coach, commenting on departed Kentucky hoops legend Adolph Rupp during what would become his inaugural, National Championship season at Kentucky*

"Adolph Rupp has won 800 and some games. Five hundred of them have been against Southeastern Conference teams. That's like me going down to Texas with six kids from Canada and starting a hockey league."
- Johnny Dee, Notre Dame basketball coach

"My God, what is it?"
- Adolph Rupp, Kentucky basketball coach upon smelling a dead skunk underneath his chair during a game against Mississippi State

"If you have grown up or have been associated with Kentucky basketball like I have, you understand the deep attachment the state and all of its fans have for their program. There is no more fervent or loyal follower than the Kentucky fan. The University of Kentucky is the essence of college basketball, and it is all that we admire—a positive tradition, an enduring passion and unparalleled success."
- Larry Conley, former Rupp's Runt, 1966

"If the United States can be called a body...then Kentucky can be called its heart." - *Jesse Stuart, Kentucky Author*

"They fought like wildcats." - *Commandant Carbusier, then head of the military department, to a group of students in a chapel service following a 6-2 football victory at Illinois on October 9, 1909. "Wildcats" became synonymous with UK thereafter*

"Baseball is a traditional sport...Our Stadium offers both fans and players a genuine baseball atmosphere. It certainly has outstanding aesthetics and tremendous personality and character." - *Coach Keith Madison on baseball at Cliff Hagan Stadium*

"When Coach Bryant walked into the locker room I always had the urge to stand up and cheer. Seeing that face for the first time--granite firm, grim, full of grit--I thought, 'This must be what God looks like.'" - *George Blanda, Kentucky football player*

"An estimated 500 ladies and gentlemen watched the game. The head-on collisions between the players were equal to the explosion of Spanish bulls crashing into one another." - *The Lexington Daily Transcript reporting of the first football game in the South at the University of Kentucky on April 9, 1880*

"You are a tall one aren't you?"

- Prince Charles of Wales, upon greeting 6'-6" Art Still after a 33-0 defeat of the Georgia Bulldogs in October, 1977

"Cawood was a dear friend for 33 years. He was a valuable member of our athletics family and was the link between our football and basketball programs and our fans for 39 years -- not only in the state of Kentucky, but nationwide. He was the epitome of recognizable class, a true gentleman." *- Larry Ivy University of Kentucky's Director of Athletics, on the passing of the Voice of the Kentucky Wildcats, Cawood Ledford*

"I am deeply saddened by the silencing of this legendary 'Voice of the Wildcats.' But the voice of Cawood Ledford will live on in our hearts forever."
 - Charles T. Wethington, Jr. Former President, University of Kentucky

"There are only two options regarding commitment. You're either **IN** or you're **OUT**. There is no such thing as life in-between." *- Pat Riley*

"When you're playing against a stacked deck, compete even harder. Show the world how much you'll fight for the winners circle. If you do, someday the cellophane will crackle off a fresh pack, one that belongs to you, and the cards will be stacked in your favor." *- Pat Riley*

"Each Warrior wants to leave the mark of his will, his signature, on important acts he touches. This is not the voice of ego but of the human spirit, rising up and declaring that it has something to contribute to the solution of the hardest problems, no matter how vexing!" *- Pat Riley*

"In the South, college football isn't just a game. It's who we are." *- Bill Curry, Kentucky football coach*

"The collisions between the players at various times were about equal to the coming together of two Spanish bulls. The sight provoked much laughter."
- Lexington Daily Transcript, April 10, 1880, describing the first college football game played in the South

"When people looked at us Southern wives coming to those football games in six-degree weather with our well-accessorized, color-coordinated outfits, helmet hair, and painted fingernails, they stared like we were a freak show."

- Nanci Kincaid

LSU

"Pete just left me flabbergasted. He did some things with the ball tonight that even I hadn't seen him do yet." - *Press Maravich, commenting on Pete's 52 point performance against Loyola in December, 1968*

"I'm trying my hardest, but I can't have everything. I can't have the looks, the rapping ability—*and* the scoring ability—and shoot free throws. But I'm going to hit em' one day."
- *Shaquille O'Neal, 1995, after missing 11 of 15 free throws against the Los Angeles Clippers*

"I never know what the hell he's going to do. It's like watching a great work of art. Sometimes I forget I'm coaching and just sit back to wait and see what's going to happen next." - *Press Maravich, on his son, Pete*

"The Lord taught me to love everybody, but the last ones I learned to love were the sportswriters." - *Alvin Dark*

"The difference between a realist and dreamer is – A realist sees the chance for failure and the dreamer sees the chance for success." - *Dale Brown*

"You can last a little longer if you know when to hit the big licks and when to avoid them." - *Jim Taylor*

"When it was time for me to go to college, I was recruited by many coaches. Some of them tried to buy me, but Coach Brown never did and we respected him for it. He kept focused on the things that were important to me -- education and family." - *Shaquille O'Neal*

"I don't remember what clubs we went to."
- Shaquille O'Neal, answering the question of whether or not he had visited the Parthenon while in Greece

"I've won championships at every level except college and pro." *- Shaquille O'Neal*

"With all those guys in suits and ties on the bench, the sideline was beginning to look like the men's shop at Macy's."
- Dale Brown, on why he cut the size of his coaching staff

"Trying to sneak a fastball past Hank Aaron is like trying to sneak the sunrise past a rooster."
- Joe Adcock, former LSU baseball great

"Tiger Stadium in Baton Rouge on a Saturday night of football is an American phenomenon. All around us, thousands of raucous Cajuns, in from the swamps and canebrakes, were dining on jambalaya and gumbo and etoufee' and boiled crawfish. And most of them, of course, had been imbibing brawny substances for twenty-four hours at the least." - *Willie Morris*

"I would imagine I'll have to get a hair piece and plastic surgery and move to Starkville, Mississippi, in the witness protection program so no one can find me." *- Skip Bertman, commenting on the possibility that LSU will turn over as many as 40,000 Tiger Stadium seats to the Tiger Athletic Foundation to boost revenues, from the Baton Rouge Business Report, January 14, 2002*

"NASA is moving the space program to Starkville, because it has no atmosphere." – Skip Bertman

"The brook trout look—we've got it, and we've got to get rid of it."

- Nick Saban, LSU head football coach on the mindset of his players

"In Baton Rouge, the focal point of everything is Tiger football." *- Jim Corbett*

"My senior year of high school, I led Cole to an undefeated 36-0 season. Three years after meeting Dale Brown, I committed to attend Louisiana State. America found out who I was. And if they didn't know, Dick Vitale, the college basketball announcer on ESPN, told them one afternoon on national television."

- Shaq, from "Shaq Talks Back"

"I will always remember Dale Brown for his enthusiasm. There are those who say he is a put-on—they just can't believe that he can be what he professes. But I never questioned that. He amazed me because there is a lot more depth to the man. He was much more than a basketball coach." *- Legendary coach John Wooden of UCLA*

"Be as positive as you can to everyone you meet and they'll always think you're a winner." *- Charles McClendon*

"Responsibility plus accountability equals success." *- John Brady*

"I'm just a little fellow—five feet eight if I stretch—but you know, basketball is the silliest game in the world. You have ten guys and only one basketball, and if I have the ball, who can beat me?" - *Sparky Wade, former LSU basketball All-American*

"Stringggggg Music!" - *Joe Dean, former LSU basketball player, SEC commentator, Converse shoe salesman, and LSU athletic director*

"Gill Brandt told me to hire Curley Hallman, and don't look back." - *Joe Dean*

"Did you see that?!!! Are you serious!!! Dale Brown, you got a diaper dandy, baby! Welcome to LSU, Shaquille O'Neal!" - *Dick Vitale, after Shaq slammed the ball over three defenders in the McDonald's High School All-American Game, from Shaq Talks Back*

"I can really feel the crowd out there! When they yell for me, it gives me goosebumps all over...When I hear that crowd roar, I swear I go *wild, crazy*! That's what I love the most." *- Pete Maravich*

"The fans want you to win, sure; but they want to be entertained, too. Why not try both?" *- Pete Maravich*

"My dad was a huge influence on me. I imagine if he had put a wrench in my hand I would have been a great mechanic."
- Pete Maravich

"He was an American phenomenon, a stepchild of the human imagination. " *- Rich Kelley, on Pete Maravich*

"Pete does things that make you say to yourself, 'Wait a minute, let me see you do that again.'"
- Ed Macauley, basketball great, on Maravich's abilities

"I played six to 10 hours a day, every day, 90 days during the summer, and I'd do incredible things. I would dribble blindfolded in the house, in the rain, and outside of moving cars. I would take my basketball to bed with me, I'd lay there after my mother kissed and tucked me in, and I'd shoot the ball up in the air and say, 'Finger tip control, backspin, follow through.'" *- The "Pistol"*

"He could do things with a basketball that I've never seen anybody do." *- Warriors great Rick Barry regarding Maravich*

"He can play basketball and I would like to have him...
I don't know of any way to guard a guy like that...The
boy is as near the complete basketball player you'll see
anywhere... If we had Pete, we'd give that West Coast
(UCLA) bunch a run for their money...I don't mind saying
I was glad to see him graduate. We were able to go
back to concentrating on how to stop *human* shooters."
   - *"The Baron," Adolph Rupp, on Pete Maravich*

"LSU already had me hooked. The other schools all tried
to recruit me with the same pitch: 'You're gonna be
blah, blah, blah." But Dale Brown told me straight up—
"Look, you might play at LSU. We got Chris Jackson
and we got Stanley Roberts right now. You *might* play."
   - *Shaq, excerpted from "Shaq Talks Back"*

"If I could build a time machine I would set it to go back to 1989-1992 and I would never leave...and I mean that." *- Shaquille O'Neal, commenting on his LSU playing days as his jersey was retired in December, 2000*

"You can accomplish a lot if you don't worry about who gets the credit." *- Bill Arnsparger, LSU football coach*

"Those were great years at LSU. They were such great years. I couldn't have asked for anything better than my four years at LSU. I received my degree in Business, played the sport I loved and made so many friends."
- Bob Pettit, commenting on his college days at the "Ole War Skule"

"The greatest thing that ever happened to me is that when I first picked up a basketball I was terrible. If things come naturally, you might not bother to work at improving them and you can fall short of your potential." - *Bob Pettit Jr., former LSU All-American and NBA All-Pro*

"There's no easier way to make a living than a pro athlete. Then, all of a sudden, you wake up and realize you have to go to work for a living." - *Bob Pettit*

"He crammed a hundred years of life into 40 years, but many lives have been positively affected because of him."

- *Julius "Dr. J." Irving on Pistol Pete Maravich*

"For a guy to go 10 years in the NBA and have a congenital anomaly like that is, to say the least, very unusual...How could a guy like that run up and down the court for 20 years?"
- Dr. Paul Thompson of Brown University on Pistol Pete Maravich, to the Associated Press after an autopsy revealed that he had a congenital anomaly his entire life that had rendered him with only half of the heart capacity of regular humans

"Tulane is the Columbia of the South." *- Ruffin Rodrigue, former LSU offensive lineman describing the Tigers' arch-rival on Willow Street in New Orleans*

"You have to play sports like there's a knife to your throat." *– Skip Bertman, to LSU tennis coach Jerry Simmons*

"His speed is deceptive. He's even slower than he looks."
- Skip Bertman describing the heavy-footed nature of one of his players

"Who's the loneliest man in Starkville?
The Tooth Fairy." *- Smoke Laval, LSU baseball coach*

"The floor we've got was built for 6-footers, not for athletes over six four or five. Today, we've got over 100 seven-footers and we're long overdue in making adjustments. It is so crowded out there that it's almost war."
- Press Maravich, LSU basketball coach, on enlarging the court

"Officiating should be developed into a career, with a college degree required." *- Press Maravich, LSU basketball coach*

"It's the best college atmosphere I've ever seen. They've got an Omaha crowd, except all of the fans are behind them."
- Tennessee Coach Rod Delmonico on playing LSU in Alex Box Stadium

"Money can buy you everything but happiness. It can pay your fare to everywhere but heaven. 'I also found out if you seek pleasure and happiness you'll never find it. But if you have the wisdom and obedience to seek Jesus Christ, happiness will find you. In the past if someone had offered me a million dollars, I would have chosen it and celebrated because of all the things I could do and all the things I could have. I've never known anyone who would turn down a million bucks. But on the other hand, God has been trying to give eternal life, totally free, and most people have rejected the offer, saying, 'I'll take the million. You can keep eternal life.'"
- Pete Maravich, excerpted from "Heir To A Dream," by Darrel Campbell

"Starkville is an Indian word for trailer park."
- Skip Bertman

"The first aluminum bats were different. They were heavier, and I can recall that several of them cracked when we used them. Those bats were nothing like the high-tech stuff the boys play with today." - *Wally McMakin, 1974 LSU baseball player*

"The bureaucrats at the NCAA are charged with researching the potency of the bats, but no one has really been talking about the baseball itself. The baseball, like the bats, is probably a little more lively than it has been in the past, but of course, no games have ever been decided because of it."

- Skip Bertman, from "SEC Baseball History & Tradition" by Chris Warner

"The battle between hitter and pitcher is one-on-one. No one can block. No picks can be set. You can't hold the ball and run out the clock. Every batter must be given their full turn at the plate." - *Warren Morris*

"In Starkville there is only one beauty parlor, and they only give estimates." - *Skip Bertman*

"I've always believed that anything you vividly image, ardently desire, sincerely believe and enthusiastically act upon must, absolutely must, come to pass." - *Skip Bertman*

"Today you not only represent yourselves, but your family, your maker, and your university. So go out and play like champions." - *Skip Bertman, prior to every LSU baseball game*

"I always saw us winning. I could see LSU going to Omaha for the College World Series. Long before we actually won the national championship in 1991, I saw it happening." *- Skip Bertman*

"I tell our players, 'Whatever you want, if you really can see it, the clearer the better, if you really believe you're worthy of it and your desire is great, if you grit your teeth when you say the word ardently, and if you act upon it everyday, enthusiastically, and make the wisest decisions you can, then it's going to happen.'" *- Skip Bertman*

"You've got to believe in yourself and your vision. The importance and power of visualization is a very, very big thing."
- Skip Bertman

"The concept of team play must be initiated from the very first day of practice. It then must be reinforced day after day after day." - *Skip Bertman*

"It's two words, plain and simple--Skip Bertman. There's no other way to explain it. Probably nobody could have done what Skip has done in such a short period of time but Skip himself."
  - *Florida State head coach Mike Martin*

"Any pitcher who throws at a batter and deliberately tries to hurt him is a communist." - *Alvin Dark, former all-around LSU athlete from the early 1940s*

"Coaching college baseball is very exciting, but it's also dangerous. You can recruit a great team but get hurt in the draft. And if two players don't play up to their potential, you're just another team." - *Skip Bertman*

"Simply put, success in LSU football is essential for the success of Louisiana State University."
- Mark Emmert, LSU Chancellor, upon the announcement that Nick Saban would be the next head football coach at LSU with a salary of $1.2 million, five times that of his as the university's top official

"There's a certain tingling sensation which develops over Tiger Stadium when the lights go on to signify another appearance of the Fighting Tigers of LSU under the darkened Louisiana skies. It has been described as a combination of Mardi Gras, the Colliseum during Rome's halcyon days, an early-day Fourth of July celebration, New Year's Eve in Times Square, and Saturn Three blasting off from its pad at Cape Kennedy." *- LSU Media Guide*

"Baton Rouge happens to be the worst place in the world to be a visiting team. It's a dugout arena, and you get all of that noise. It's like being inside of a drum."

- Coach Paul "Bear" Bryant on the experience of Tiger Stadium

"It's always nice to take a trip to Louisiana. Unfortunately, we have to play a football game while we're down there." *- Akron University's football coach, on the eve of the team's 56-0 loss to Louisiana State University in Death Valley in Baton Rouge*

"The wild excitement inside Tiger Stadium is shattering. It's like an electric wire running from the stands to the field."

- LSU Head Coach Charles McClendon on Tiger Stadium

"I'd rather face the lions in the Coliseum than the Tigers in Baton Rouge."
- *Bobby Dodd*

"I don't fool around with losers! LSU can't have a losing football team, because that will mean that I am associated with a loser!" - *Louisiana Governor Huey Long*

"...My God, my God, I have so much left to do. Who will look after my darling LSU?" - *Huey Long's last words*

"The athletic field is very democratic. Each person is judged by personal merit rather than personal wealth or prestige."- *Paul Dietzel*

LSU

"I like to throw the ball. To me, the pro game is throwing. I may be wrong, but putting the ball in the air is the way to win." - *Y.A. Tittle*

"We came to win, not to tie. If I had it to do over a hundred times, I would do the same thing." - *Paul Dietzel, after a two-point conversion failed resulting in a 14-13 loss to Tennessee. The loss ended LSU's 19-game winning streak*

"There are no office hours for champions." - *Paul Dietzel*

"The worst mistake any coach can make is not being himself."
- *Charles McClendon*

"In Baton Rouge, it's not a law to love LSU, but the city fathers could probably get one passed if they needed to."
- *Charles McClendon*

"Everybody at LSU wants another great team like '58. The only trouble is that our schedule is so tough, we could have a great year and never know it." - *Charles McClendon*

"Outside the Louisiana Purchase in 1803, many Cajuns consider Billy Cannon's run the greatest event in state history."
- *Mississippi Head Coach John Vaught, regarding Billy Cannon's magical romp*

"What you find in Baton Rouge is typical of the football frenzy in the South. No city in the country hath greater love for its football team. So deep is the feeling that workers arrange vacations, night shifts, bowling leagues, weddings and even family pregnancies so that they won't conflict with LSU games." - *John D. McCallum on football at LSU*

"It's a magical setting, the excitement, the atmosphere, is unmatched anywhere -- and I've been in stadiums from one end of America to the other. They ought to put up a statue to the guy who came up with night football at LSU." - *Mike Bynum, sports author*

"No scholar of the Dixie gridiron can pass his years in this mortal coil without witnessing a night game in Tiger Stadium in Baton Rouge. The sinking burnt-orange Louisiana sun casts death-like shadows upon this terrain of old tumult, and minutes before kickoff the ceaseless mounting clamor rises in synesthesia, making one feel he is in the presence of some elemental phenomenon of near geological propensity."
- *Willie Morris, The Sporting News*

"In football, and in life, you've got to keep proving yourself."
- *Charlie McClendon*

"I wouldn't. I would just go home. I'd fake an injury or something."
- *Shaquille O'Neal, (When asked how he would defend against himself)*

"It makes a body tingle. These folks go berzerk when the band marches on the field. A huge roar is heard for the invocation, for heaven's sake. They not only know the words to the national anthem, they sing them, loudly. And when the Tigers win the toss...there are tears of ecstasy." - *Douglas Looney, Sports Illustrated*

"We're kind of like the Rodney Dangerfield of the league. Fifth, sixth, it's not where you're picked but where you finish."
- *John Brady, LSU basketball coach*

"Encircling itself, high and in the air like a fortress abandoned during some particularly bloodied age, towers the most ferocious address in Louisiana. In Tiger Stadium, a game is not merely seen. It is HEARD. The sound of it twists up the steel and concrete enclosure like a particularly sinister tornado. The parts are played out equally in the stands and on the field. Writers in the press box, high over the crowd, find themselves unable to think when the noise stops. If it stops." *-John Logue*

"I'd like to be there when the BCS tries to sort this one out."

- Josh Reed, LSU Biletnikoff Award winner, after ruining UT's Rose Bowl chances by defeating the heavily-favored Vols in the SEC Championship Game in Atlanta, 2001

"I want my family, players and friends to only share tears of happiness today. Let's all remember the good times while we were together. I have prayed that what little I could contribute to our society would help make the place we live a little better. I challenge my family, players and friends who I love so much to do the same thing. You can do it. Love your family and neighbors as I have loved mine. Commit yourself to do something good for others. My last coaching point: teach the world that the word 'responsibility' means 'your actions.'" - *Charles McClendon, terminally ill with cancer, Tiger Stadium Memorial service, Florida game, 2001*

"We were cordial. 'Hey, how you doing, good to see you' type thing. But it's not like we went out and had a whiskey." - *LSU head basketball coach John Brady on whether or not he and Alabama head basketball coach Mike Gottfried spoke at a function in the French Quarter prior to the 2001 Sugar Bowl Classic in New Orleans*

"Some may find this hard to believe, but some of my best times for me as a basketball player at LSU were before each game we played. Coach Brown would prepare us mentally for the contest by telling these incredibly animated stories, most of them being motivational in nature. After Coach Brown spoke, we would all stand and hold hands in a circle to say the Lord's prayer. This was the defining moment in each game for the LSU basketball team. It gave us that bond that allowed us to trust and have confidence in each other. After this pregame ritual had been fulfilled, and we ran out on the floor, I am not sure if any of us even felt our legs moving beneath us."

- Ricky Blanton, former LSU basketball standout, excerpted from the foreword of "SEC Basketball History & Tradition," by Chris Warner

"If you're looking back, you're in trouble."

- Charles McClendon

"I got a hand on him, but he just shook me off like a puppy." *- Jake Gibbs, Ole Miss defender describing his futile attempt to tackle the eventual Heisman Trophy winner, Billy Cannon, in Tiger Stadium on Halloween night, 1959*

"Entering Louisiana—Please Set your clocks back four seconds." *- Placard that was erected on the Louisiana-Mississippi border within days of the historic gridiron contest between LSU and Ole Miss in 1972, which Ole Miss fans claim was stolen by the Tiger timekeeper*

"I have been blessed to have been associated with some outstanding people and been fortunate to coach and a be a part of so many young men's lives." *- LSU coach Pete Jenkins, on his retirement from coaching in February, 2002*

"There is no single "best" way to do something in football."
- *Charles McClendon*

"I think a kicker's job is to make sure his name is not mentioned. If it is in the paper, it usually is not a good thing."
- *LSU kicker John Corbello*

"What looked exciting from the stands was really just mud, blood and sweat." - *Tommy Casanova, three-time All-American LSU safety, excerpted from the foreword of "A Tailgater's Guide To SEC Football"*

"It's a sad thought in knowing I won't ever run through those goal posts anymore. I can still picture the first time I ran out in Tiger Stadium. It was kind of eerie. I looked around a couple of times…Boy! What a thrill that was. That was some thrill." - *Pete Jenkins, LSU assistant coach, upon his retirement in the spring of 2002*

"It didn't matter if he was big or small, fast or slow, All-American or second team, my job was to beat him and beat him soundly." *- Tommy Casanova, three-time All-American, on his approach to the game of football*

"Even when it's two outs in the bottom of the ninth, you just have to believe." *- Warren Morris, from the foreword of the book, "SEC Baseball History & Tradition," by Chris Warner*

"Huey Long said a chicken in every pot, not a ticket in every pot."

- Skip Bertman, LSU athletic director, 2001, commenting on the public outcry against impending ticket surcharges for LSU football tickets, even though LSU was the only school within the conference yet to implement the necessary revenue-generating measure

"One will not find the true fiber of a man in times of prosperity or success, but only in his resiliency and attitude through times of failure."
- Dale Brown

"I can't coach everyone. Someone quoted me as saying that I can only coach certain kinds of players...I think that's true. Only certain types of players can reach their capacity under me. If a player is not committed to excellence...if he is not interested in being part of a family concept...if he is only interested in himself...if all he cares about is polishing his skills so he can make a lot of money in the NBA, then he probably shouldn't play for me." *- Dale Brown*

"Always do your best, never give up, and let God take care of the rest." *- Dale Brown*

"Pride in the strength of sectional football teams took its place along with pride in the valor of the Confederate army as a major source of Southern chauvinism. Athletes became glamorous new Southern heroes, and their coach the best-known university figure to the general populace."

- Francis Butler Simkins and Charles Rolands,
from their book, A History of the South

Mississippi State

"Football is a lot like engineering, if you work long and hard enough you can come up with the answer to the problem."
- *Charlie Shira, Mississippi State football coach*

"Every coach in the country ought to thank the Lord for ESPN when we say our prayers at night."
- *Mississippi State coach Ron Polk, on ESPN's extensive pioneering coverage of college baseball*

"You tell them what the score is, who has the ball, and how much time's left, and cut out all that other bulls**t."
- *Dudy Noble, instructing Jack Cristil on how to call ball games*

"Luck is what happens when preparation meets opportunity."
- *Darrell Royal, Mississippi State football coach*

"Ron Polk and the Bulldogs are lucky to have such great fan support. Our players aren't used to the size crowds that they draw here, and they're not used to having such knowledgeable fans, either. I mean, these people really know the game and appreciate it. That's what is so enjoyable about playing here."
    - Gary Adams, UCLA baseball coach

"In 1984 and 1985, when I was in junior high, Clark, Palmerio, Thigpen and Brantley were playing here. They were my idols and I tried to imitate everything they did. It's always been a dream of mine to come here and play on the same field where they played."
    - Craig Bane, Starkville native and Bulldog designated hitter

"You can't be aggressive and confused at the same time." *- Darrell Royal*

"While we've always been a pretty good road team, it is difficult to leave the friendly confines of Dudy Noble Field. Playing in an atmosphere that is so different from what our players are used to at home can be a distraction. But, it's part of college baseball and you have to adjust to it." - *Ron Polk, Mississippi State head coach, from Inside Dudy Noble, A Celebration of MSU Baseball, by Steve Ellis*

"Football doesn't build character. It eliminates weak ones." - *Darrell Royal*

"When it gets right down to the wood-chopping, the key to winning is **confidence**." - *Darrell Royal*

"A little bit of perfume doesn't hurt you if you don't drink it." - *Darrell Royal*

"The older I became, the more I felt myself drawn back to Dudy Noble. There are many reasons. It's great baseball played by very talented kids. The game is uncorrupted by money. The place is filled by memories, both of my college days and of the great games and moments since then. It's a wonderful place to unwind. The mood is festive. Time is meaningless. The game is played without a clock. There are no telephones in Left Field. Deadlines are more distant. Appointments seem insignificant. Regardless of wins and losses, I always feel better when I leave Dudy Noble Field than when I arrive. There are few places of which this can be said."

- *John Grisham, Mississippi State Alumnus*

"Almost every one of them who called told me, 'It's time for our coach to come home,' and not one of them mentioned Ron Polk's name. When Nat Showalter, Will Clark and Rafael Palmeiro called and said, 'We want our coach back,' that's pretty strong." - *Larry Templeton*

"I've enjoyed my association with college baseball for the past nine years and if someone were to ask me why, I would have to say that the program at Mississippi State is a primary example. The kids, Ron Polk, the beautiful facility and the Left Field Lounge. Baseball in Starkville is the way it should be-warm, green grass, enthusiastic players-good family entertainment. I'm glad I've had the pleasure of experiencing it!"
- *Jim Kaat, broadcaster and former major league pitcher*

"When good things have happened over a period of years, and you expect good things to happen again—that's tradition."
- *Darrell Royal*

"The only way I know to keep football fun is to win. There is no laughter in losing." - *Darrell Royal*

"You cannot really be good without seniors who are big winners." - *Darrell Royal*

"Never try to fool a player. You can't kid a kid." - *Darrell Royal*

"Treat turnovers like a copperhead in the bedclothes; avoid them at all costs." - *Darrell Royal*

"On gameday, I'm as nervous as a pig in a packing plant." - _Darrell Royal_

"You've got to be in a position for luck to happen. Luck doesn't go around looking for a stumblebum."
     - _Darrell Royal_

"Without question, baseball has been a sport that we have been complimented on nationally for many decades. We set our goals early on for other (MSU) sports to compete at that level."
     - _Mississippi State athletic director Larry Templeton_

"As a cornerback, you can't have a conscience -- if you do have a conscience, you need to change your position to safety or something."
     - _Fred Smoot, MSU defensive back and self-proclaimed "Sultan of Smack"_

"There's no such thing as a perfect corner. Everybody has given up a pass. And if you're worrying about your last play, you aren't focused on the next one. I learned from the mistakes we made in that game. And it's not about questioning what you did wrong. How fast can you rebound is the question." - *Fred Smoot*

"I just expect more of myself, but with the Gators coming to town this weekend, I love that. I'm sure they'd love nothing more than to make me look bad. I know Steve Spurrier's that kind of coach, and I'm that kind of player. But I've got a good feeling for Saturday." - *Fred Smoot, before the Bulldogs' monumental upset win of Florida in 2000*

"Florida passes and passes and will not throw away from you. Just because I'm over here, doesn't mean that they aren't going to throw it over here. Steve Spurrier doesn't think like that. With my big mouth, he will probably want to come my way. I like that." - _Fred Smoot_

"Friends don't let friends go to Ole Miss."
- Mississippi State Fan Tee Shirt

"Has there ever been a place so lovely? A place that feels like home to so many? The lines so perfect, the grass so green, the hot dogs so good. A place that has brought us so much anticipation, exhiliration and contentment, all at one time? Dudy Noble Field, home of the baseball Bulldogs of Mississippi State University, is just such a place." _- Steve Ellis_

"When these two great schools get together in Baton Rouge or Starkville, there's no question it's going to be a great game. It is one of college sports' great rivalries."
- Skip Bertman, on the MSU – LSU baseball series

"Ron has always been the epitome of the college baseball coach. His knowledge of the game and his ability to relate with young people are only part of it. All of us in college baseball marvel at his energy and his expertise in so many areas. While the tradition at State has always been great, there's no question that Ron has raised it to a new level."
- Skip Bertman on Ron Polk

"I am convinced Starkville is one of the key cities for the federal government's Witness Protection Program. Why? Well, for starters there are over a dozen Italian restaurants there. Do the math." *- Skip Bertman*

"I guess every ballpark, in earlier times, was something else. Great things come from humble origins and all that, but it's difficult to believe Dudy Noble was once a cow pasture."
- John Grisham, Mississippi State graduate

"He (Ron Polk) won, as he always has and always will, and suddenly the stands were full, the crowds were loud, the trucks and trailers appeared in left field, the Lounge was open for business, and the clouds of barbecue smoke became a symbol of baseball success at Mississippi State University."

- *John Grisham, from the Introduction of Inside Dudy Noble, by Steve Ellis*

"All that spectators get out of the game (of football) now is fresh air, the comical articles in his program, the sight of 22 young men rushing about in mysterious formations, and whatever he brought in his flask."

- Robert Benchley

Ole Miss

"I miss football so much—heck, I even miss the interceptions." - *Archie Manning*

"The team had much discussion as to the colors that should be adopted, but it was finally suggested by the manager that the union of the crimson of Harvard and the Navy Blue of Yale would be harmonious, and that it was well to have the spirit of both of these good colleges." - *Dr. A. Bondurant, organizer and manager coach of the University of Mississippi, describing how the red and blue were adopted by the university as its official colors*

"Well, God is certainly getting an earful tonight." - *Jim Murray, sports columnist, on the death of former Rebel head baseball coach Casey Stengel*

"Going to bed with a woman never hurt a ball player. It's staying up all night looking for them that does you in." - *Casey Stengel*

"If you don't get it by midnight, chances are you aren't gonna get it, and if you do, it ain't worth it." *- Casey Stengel*

"If you walk backwards, you'll find out that you can go forward and people won't know if you're coming or going."
- Casey Stengel

"If 18 sports writers wish to use 'Rebels', I shall not rebel, so let it go Ole Miss Rebels."

- The late Judge William Hemingway of the university athletic community, on the newly-chosen moniker for the University of Mississippi athletic squads

"Good pitching will always stop good hitting and vice-versa." *- Casey Stengel*

"They didn't give him a cake. They were afraid he'd drop it."
- Casey Stengel, former Rebel coach, and baseball manager of the New York Yankees, celebrating the birthday of his notoriously weak-fielding first baseman, New York Daily News, April 23, 1981

"Leroy 'Satchell' Paige threw the ball as far from the bat and as close to the plate as possible." *- Casey Stengel*

"When you hear forty-six thousand Rebels screaming for your blood—and meaning it— it can be eerie." *- Vince Dooley*

"All my life, I have always been the underdog...When I went to high school people said, 'He was in junior high. Those kids can't play. When he gets to high school it'll be a different story.' After I left high school, people said, 'When you get to college you won't get a chance to play because you're too little, you're not quick enough, you can't shoot well enough...I just try and prove them wrong. It's like a journey."
- *Ole Miss head basketball coach, Rod Barnes*

"Growing up in Drew in the late 50s and early 60s was wonderful. It's really hard to think of a better place to grow up. We're talking about an easy, small-town way of life with friendly people who watched over you. If anybody had it better than me, I sure didn't know it."
- *Archie Manning*

"I looked up the information on the guy who was going to be across from me. He was an All-American candidate named Joe Rushing. He outweighed me by 25 pounds, was 26 years old, married with four kids and had been to Vietnam. I said, "Uh oh.'" - *Skipper Jernigan, teammate of Archie Manning prior to their first varsity game as Rebels*

"Not a bit; we lose at any altitude."

- Former Ole Miss baseball coach Casey Stengel, when asked if Mexico City's altitude bothered his players after the Mexico City Red Devils beat his Mets 6-4

"Football is the essence of America, but not because of championships or titles. The drive to compete—the guts to play—the will to come from behind—the grace to walk off the field a loser—that's the essence of football." - *Archie Manning*

"Bad teams are creative. They always find a new way to lose." *- Archie Manning*

"No matter how bad things seem, never give up…"
- Chucky Mullins

"You'll never know how much God means to you, till tragedy hits and friends come through." *- Chucky Mullins*

"Let them revive the spitter and help the pitchers make a living." *- Casey Stengel, former Ole Miss baseball coach*

"I don't like them fellas who drive in two runs and let in three." *- Casey Stengel*

"In a very fine atmosphere in a grand old university."
    - Casey Stengel, "The Professor of Baseball" referring to the University of Mississippi in Oxford

"Managing is getting paid for home runs someone else hits." *- Casey Stengel*

"Recruiting has become a spectator sport, and it's a free seat." *- Mississippi Coach David Cutcliffe*

"An Ole Miss football game in Oxford is a trip in a time machine. A trip backward." *- Lewis Grizzard*

"They still wave the flag, still sing 'Dixie,' they can still pray and they can still bring liquor into the game. No wonder they beat us."
- *Bugar Seely, a veteran Georgia fan, on Ole Miss*

"Two hundred million Americans, and there ain't two good catchers among 'em." - *Casey Stengel*

"Most games are lost, not won." - *Casey Stengel*

"The secret to managing is to keep the guys who hate you away from the guys who are undecided." - *Casey Stengel*

"If you ain't ready to play after walking through the Grove, you're probably dead." *- Billy Brewer*

"Discipline, with team togetherness, wins football games." *- Johnny Vaught*

"When I talk to kids about football, I talk to them about having fun." *- Archie Manning*

"The worst thing a coach can do is stand pat and think the things that worked yesterday will win tomorrow. Intelligent changes must be made." *- Johnny Vaught*

"I was walking through the campus and I saw fraternity boys in coats and ties with their dates, who were in heels. Then, I heard somebody playing 'Dixie' on a trumpet. I kept looking around for Michael J. Fox in 'Back to the Future.'"
- Unknown Georgia fan, describing the scene on gameday in Oxford

"I consider a tie a loss." *- Johnny Vaught*

"The athletic fever has now taken full possession of the University...and the time is already here when, in order to rank high in college or society, one must join the running crowd and play on the football team." *- James "Bobo" Champion, Ole Miss, 1893*

"There is a valid distinction between The University and Ole Miss even though the separate threads are closely interwoven. The University is buildings, trees and people. Ole Miss is mood, emotion and personality. One is physical, and the other is spiritual. One is tangible, and the other intangible. The University is respected, but Ole Miss is loved. The University gives a diploma and regretfully terminates tenure, but one never graduates from Ole Miss." - *Frank E. Everett, Jr., B.A. 1932, LLB 1934*

"To be a winning team, you must be a hungry team. So remember that every football Saturday is the most important date on the schedule." - *Johnny Vaught*

"You can't have a miracle every day—except you can when you get great pitching." - *Casey Stengel*

"He's 19 years old and in 10 years he's got a chance to be 29." *- Casey Stengel on a prospect*

"Left-handers have more enthusiasm for life. They sleep on the wrong side of the bed, and their heads get more stagnant on that side." *- Casey Stengel*

"If that young fella was running for office in Israel, they'd have a whole new government over there, and he'd boss it just like he bosses practically every game he pitches." *- Casey Stengel, on Sandy Koufax*

"They examined all my organs. Some of them are quite remarkable, and others are not so good. Several museums are bidding on them." *- Casey Stengel*

"Let them hit you. I'll get you a new neck."
- Casey Stengel, offering advice to a player

"Old-timers' games, weekends, and airplane landings are alike. If you can walk away from them, they're successful." *- Casey Stengel*

"He doesn't drink, he doesn't smoke, he doesn't chew, he doesn't stay out late, and he still can't hit .250." *- Casey Stengel, on a straight-laced player*

"Take those fellows over to the other diamond—I want to see if they can play on the road."
- *Casey Stengel, on an intrasquad practice*

"The trick is growing up without getting old."
- *Casey Stengel*

"They'll have to carry me out of here in a pine box."
- *Tommy Tuberville, proclaiming his steadfast allegiance to Ole Miss right before taking the head coaching job at Auburn*

"We're in such a slump that even the ones that are drinkin' aren't hittin'."
- *Casey Stengel*

"I can tell you in just a heartbeat what my fascination with sports is. It's this: I think all of us are looking for that which does not admit of bullshit. You can't get it in a marriage, you can't get it in a –to use a word I hate— relationship, you can't get it from the church or the government."

- Harry Crews

South Carolina

"One day, Derek will either be filling up NFL stadiums, or sweeping them up."
- Lou Holtz, South Carolina football coach, describing former Gamecock running back Derek Watson

"My wife wanted a big diamond."
- Mookie Wilson, former South Carolina standout, explaining why he was wed in a ballpark

"It's not the load that breaks you down, it's the way you carry it." *- Lou Holtz*

"Only the unprepared are overcome by pressure." *- Lou Holtz*

"My grandmother raised nine kids of her own and three of my mother's. I'm a reflection of both my grandmother and my brother, Sterling, I owe it all to them."

- Shannon Sharpe, brother of former Gamecock standout, Sterling Sharpe

"The difference between involvement and commitment can be illustrated by the story of the kamikaze pilot who flew 20 missions. He was involved, but he wasn't committed."

- *Lou Holtz*

-

"I'll never learn anything talking. I only learn things when I ask questions." - *Lou Holtz*

"The only time you can start at the top is when you're digging a hole." - *Lou Holtz*

"Life is really exciting. One day you're drinking the wine, and the next day you're picking the grapes." - *Lou Holtz*

"Show me someone who has done something worthwhile, and I'll show you someone who has overcome adversity."
   - Lou Holtz

"We have the greatest fans in the world. We raise more money per win than any school in America."
   - Lou Holtz, South Carolina head coach

"I can't believe God put us on this earth to be ordinary." - *Lou Holtz*

"Any time your defense gives up more points than your basketball team, you're in trouble." - *Lou Holtz*

"First we will be best, then we will be first." - *Lou Holtz*

"When all is said and done, more is said than done." - *Lou Holtz*

"A gamecock is a feisty, fighting rooster known for its spirit, its courage and its capacity to fight to the very end." - *South Carolina Athletic Department*

"Here's A Health, Carolina."

- Popular Gamecock alumni toast

"The ancient Syrians worshiped the fighting cock as one of
their deities. In China, the gamecock is considered the
herald of mortal existence and a symbol of honor, merit, and
the west. In ancient Greece, the gamecock was the
announcer of the sun and was considered sacred because of
its magnanimity, courage, skill, and constancy. In Germany
and Hungary, the gamecock is still considered a weather
prophet. Over the centuries, such noble attributes have been
associated with the gamecock as diligence, wakefulness,
defiance, and vigilance." *- John M. Palms, devout Gamecock fan*

"Don't be a spectator. Don't let life pass you by." *- Lou Holtz*

"The best teams have their fans in the stands an hour before kickoff."
- Brad Scott, South Carolina football coach

"Motivation is simple. You eliminate those who aren't motivated." *- Lou Holtz*

"Difficulties in life are intended to make us better, not bitter." *- Dan Reeves, former South Carolina standout*

"You never get comfortable in this game."
  - Dan Reeves on football

"George Rogers was the nicest guy you would ever want to meet. He also happened to be the best player we ever had."
  - Bob Fulton

"The man who complains about the way the ball bounces is likely the one who dropped it." *- Lou Holtz*

"Self-discipline is an individual's greatest asset."
  - Lou Holtz

"You live up—or down—to your expectations." *- Lou Holtz*

"There's nothing in this world more instinctively abhorrent to me than finding myself in agreement with my fellow humans." - *Lou Holtz*

"Folks in South Carolina are not just great fans, they're great people." - *Bob Fulton*

"I want to rush for 1,000 or 1,500 yards, whichever comes first."

- *New Orleans Saint (former South Carolina Gamecock) RB George Rogers*

"Regardless of whether you play well or not, you show class when you come from behind." - *Paul Dietzel*

"We wouldn't be allowed on Noah's Ark because we don't have two of everything."

- Lou Holtz

"If you don't make a total commitment to whatever you're doing, then you start looking to bail out the first time the boat starts leaking. It's tough enough getting that boat to shore with everybody rowing, let alone when a guy stands up and starts putting his jacket on." _- Lou Holtz_

"All winning teams are goal-oriented. Teams like these win consistently because everyone connected with them concentrates on specific objectives. They go about their business with blinders on; nothing will distract them from achieving their aims."_- Lou Holtz_

"I think everyone should experience defeat at least once during their career. You learn a lot from it." *- Lou Holtz*

"I love to listen to Bo talk. Maybe it's because I don't have much choice when we're together."
- Lou Holtz, on Big Ten legend Bo Schembechler

"The best way to save face is by keeping the lower part of it shut." *- Lou Holtz*

"Absolutely. There are a thousand better coaches in the cities, but I'm the best in the country."
- Lou Holtz, on whether he agrees with those who call him the best coach in the country

"I won't accept anything less than the best a player's capable of doing...and he has the right to expect the best that I can do for him and the team!" - *Lou Holtz*

"Ability is what you're capable of doing. Motivation determines what you do. Attitude determines how well you do it." - *Lou Holtz*

"She was wrong. By the end of the season I'd sold our stereo, our car, her jewels, and our television."

- Lou Holtz, on a part-time job selling cemetery plots even though his wife told him he couldn't sell anything

"How you respond to the challenge in the second half will determine what you become after the game, whether you are a winner or a loser." *- Lou Holtz*

"We aren't where we want to be, we aren't where we ought to be, but thank goodness we aren't where we used to be!" *- Lou Holtz*

"In the South, football is creatively confused with religion, chivalry, the Civil War and women."

- Diane Roberts

Tennessee

"My college experience was a really good one, so I decided to stay all four years. I just didn't want to look back and say I wish I would have stayed my senior year. That's really what it was in a nutshell. I just kind of wanted to be a senior in college. I had already completed my degree in three years, so, I knew I had a chance to slow things down a little bit. I had the opportunity to really take everything in and create a lot of memories for myself and I'm certainly glad I did. For months I was asked the same question repeatedly every day: 'Why did you *really* stay?' I just wanted to enjoy being a college senior. For some reason people had a very hard time believing that."
- *Peyton Manning*

"Tennessee is Tennessee and rich in tradition."
- *Frank Broyles*

"If the Russians had a football team, maybe I'd rather beat them than Tennessee." *- Chuck Fairbanks, Oklahoma Sooner head coach, after his team lost to the Vols in the Orange Bowl in 1968*

"The infectious germ of being a winner." *- Malcolm Aitken, captain of the 1932 Vols, when asked what he remembered most about Tennessee football*

"A squad can become bloated with victory upon victory. An occasional defeat is a fine alkalizer." *- Fred Russell, sports editor, Nashville Banner, January 2, 1940, after undefeated and unscored upon 1939 Vols lost to Southern California 14-0 in the Rose Bowl*

"The biggest myth about Southern women is that they wear too much makeup." *- Peyton Manning*

"I'll be a Volunteer the rest of my life." *- Peyton Manning*

"The best move I ever made."
- Dean Nathan Daugherty on hiring Robert Reese Neyland

"I was like this great big sponge while Peyton was here, soaking up everything I could." *- Tee Martin*

"There won't be any way to estimate what Reggie meant to us. It's inestimable. He provided humor, leadership, morale." *- Johnny Majors, on the graduation loss of Reggie White in 1984*

"Knock a man down, and if you can't, step aside and let me through." *- Gene McEver, 1929 All-American; considered to be the greatest football player to ever wear the orange and white of Tennessee*

"The more I am involved with football, the more I believe that emotions determine the outcome of most games...How ready a team is to play is sometimes everything." *- Bob Johnson*

"Intercollegiate basketball will make its initial appearance in Knoxville tonight when in the YMCA gymnasium at the University of Tennessee, the Volunteers will meet the five hailing from the Central University of Kentucky at Danville."
- Ben Byrd, Knoxville Journal and Tribune, Thursday, December 16, 1909

"Here, where the hills are high, Tennessee fans are calling on the Volunteers to give the state its first clear claim to national honors. Knoxville is the perfect example of civil lunacy. Every suburb is a wing of an asylum."
- Henry McLemore, UPI, Halloween, 1939

"To play for Tennessee, you've got to get wet all over."
- Leonard Coffman, Tennessee fullback, 1937-39

"Tennessee football is Tennessee."
- Former Tennessee Governor, Winfield Dunn

"At Tennessee, our fans expect us to win all our games all the time. It's unrealistic, but that's the way it is." *- Phil Fulmer*

"College football doesn't get any bigger than Tennessee." *- Casey Clausen*

"The game of football is beginning to gain a foothold in Knoxville." *- The Knoxville Journal, 1891*

"On a crisp mid-October Saturday, you could climb a hill and, if the wind was just right, you could hear the rich people booing Bear Bryant and the Tide." - *Jake Vest, Orlando Sentinel*

"Our band plays Rocky Top at least 20 times a game, although our opponents would put that number closer to one hundred."
- Bud Ford, University of Tennessee Athletics

"I'll live today the rest of my life."

- Scrappy Moore, Chatanooga football coach, after defeating the Tennessee Vols for the first time in 51 years

"Football is bigger than the university now—it's the tail that wags the dog. That wasn't the case when we played."

- Andy Kozar, from "Bragging Rights" by Richard Ernsberger

"If teaching athletes the importance of education ruins the football program, then the football program does not belong in the university."
- *Linda Bensel-Meyers, University of Tennessee professor*

"Taking the shortest distance to the ball carrier and arriving in bad humor."
- *Bowden Wyatt, Tennessee football coach, on pursuit*

"Our bench is kind of like a video store on a Saturday night—there aren't a lot of choices." - *Kevin O'Neill, Tennessee basketball coach, on the depth of his team, which had been plagued by injuries*

"Baseball is such a marvelous spectator sport. And one of the joys of the game is that it can be pursued to any depth that one desires. You can watch a game superficially, enjoy it as entertainment, and carry on a conversation with a friend at the same time. Or, if you choose, you can watch in the manner of a chess match, considering the ramifications of every pitch." *- Former Tennessee broadcaster Lindsey Nelson from "Hello Everybody, I'm Lindsey Nelson"*

"No head coach can be better than his staff. Show me a winning team, and I'll show you a good group of assistant coaches." *- Johnny Majors*

"There soon developed a great spectator interest. Crowds of students and friends began following the teams. Identifying themselves with the contestants, they enjoyed an afternoon of jubilation or great agony, depending on the fortunes of their favorite team. Older men and women became as excited as the students. Players carried their coaches off the field when they won, and many of them were observed weeping when they lost. By the mid-1890s sportswriters were having a field day. They had a game that stretched their abilities to describe, and they had an audience that was calling for more. Football was becoming more than a college sport; it was becoming the talk and interest of the town."

- Nathan W. Dougherty, University of Tennessee Engineering professor and author of "Educators and Athletes," 1976, describing the development of the game of football in the South prior to the turn of the twentieth century

"Because the NCAA has a vested interest in keeping profitable collegiate teams viable, using the NCAA to oversee academics within the Athletics Department makes as much sense as letting the fox protect the chicken farm."
- *Linda Bensel-Myers, University of Tennessee educator*

"The records trace the fracturing of a student's hopes and dreams: how an ambitious, though academically disadvantaged, student who buys into the myth of the athletics scholarship as a way to better himself fares when confronted with the economic self-interest of the institution."
- *Linda Bensel-Meyers*

"It is clear that the integrity of the system continues to decline, and that the Athletics Department is mandating unacceptable tutoring practices that can only be described as institutional plagiarism." - *Linda Bensel-Meyers*

"...No matter where I was broadcasting from, I found the fans in the South to be knowledgeable, fair--and yes, loud and frenzied. They are very proud of their rich football heritage. And they are very proud of their schools, their teams--and the deep pride that goes with being from the South."
- *George Mooney, the "Voice of the Volunteers" on radio during the 1950's*

"The lessons learned upon the football field are carried usefully on to the field of life." - *General Robert Neyland*

"A football team is like an army. Your men must be in good physical condition. They must have technical ability, and they must have high morale." - *General Robert Neyland*

"To defeat a weak opponent is not the problem: The problem is to win when he is as good or better than you."
- *General Robert Neyland*

"Class is, when they run you out of town, you look like you're leading a parade." *- Bill Battle, Tennessee football coach*

"It's football time in Tennessee!" *- John Ward*

"The 10, 5, 4, 3, 2, 1. Give him six. Touchdown Tennessee!"
- John Ward

"The kick is up. Ladies and gentleman, that kick is good!"
- John Ward

"John Ward is more important to Tennessee football than any player or coach we've ever had. From the time I was a little boy, he was Tennessee football. He was the man we trusted." *- Tennessee placekicker, Jeff Hall*

"The general was always in complete control. He never got excited. He was highly organized and a great disciplinarian." *- John Michaels, Tennessee player, 1949-52 on General Robert Neyland*

"The general was not the easiest guy to work with Monday through Friday, but on Saturday he was a fatherly figure. On Saturday he was a warm man who gave you a lot of confidence."
- Herky Payne, Tennessee Vol, 1949-51, on General Neyland

"Proper mental attitude on game day stems almost entirely from attitudes built up over a considerable period of time. Pregame harangues, as a rule, do more harm than good. Inspiration at zero hour is a poor thing to rely on." *- General Robert Neyland*

"The team that makes the fewest mistakes wins." — *Robert Neyland*

"Homosexuality is a decision, not a race. People from all different ethnic backgrounds are living this lifestyle. But people from all different backgrounds are liars and cheaters and malicious backstabbers." *- Reggie White, 1998, ordained minister, former Tenneseee Volunteer, in a speech to the Wisconsin State Assembly, denouncing homosexuality as 'one of the biggest sins of the Bible'*

"When you look at the black race, black people are very gifted in what we call worship and celebration. A lot of us like to dance, and if you go to a black church, you see people jumping up and down because they really get into it." *- Reggie White, 1998*

"White people are blessed with the gift of structure and organization. You guys do a good job with building business and things of that nature. And you know how to tap into money pretty much better than a lot of people around the world."
- *Reggie White, 1998*

"Hispanics are gifted in family structure. You see a Hispanic person, and they can put 20 or 30 people in one home." - *Reggie White, 1998*

"When you look at the Asian, the Asian is very gifted in creativity and invention. If you go to Japan or to any Asian country, they can turn a television into a watch. Like I said, they are very creative." - *Reggie White, 1998*

"Southerners are proud of their football heritage, their schools, and their teams. And they share a deep pride that goes with being from the South."
- George Mooney, Voice of the Volunteers

"Football is a game of defense and field position."
- General Robert Neyland

"If you win, you win doing the things you do best."
- Doug Dickey

"Wealth and status mean nothing on the football field; effort and unselfishness mean everything." *- Johnny Majors*

"In the struggle between equal teams, the difference is never physical but invariably mental." - *General Robert Neyland*

"What makes for success? Practice. We scrimage plays more than 100 times in the fall. You don't develop good teeth eating mush, and you don't learn good football going through the motions." - *General Robert Neyland*

"Practice doesn't make perfect. Perfect practice makes perfect."
- *Johnny Majors*

"When they look back at that 9-1 season, they don't ask who the nine were." - *General Robert Neyland*

"He told me that whenever he is feeling down and out, he just watches the videotape of that game. And it made him feel better. That's how much that one game meant to the Tennessee people."
- Johnny Majors, Tennessee coach, on a chance encounter with a Tennessee fan who explained how moved he was by Tennessee's 35-7 upset of highly-ranked Miami in 1986

"Tennessee sophomores don't deserve citizenship papers until they have survived an Alabama game."
- General Robert Neyland

"People who haven't been to Knoxville on a football Saturday can't understand the experience. It's excitement beyond description." *- Bob Bell*

"It is important to keep the squad eternally aware of the very nature of football so that they are not dismayed when things are going wrong."
- General Robert Neyland

"You never know what a football player is made of until he plays Alabama." *- General Robert Neyland*

"To be good, a team must have good seniors."
- Johnny Majors

"The first thing any coaching staff must do is weed out selfishness. No program can be successful with players who put themselves ahead of the team." *- Johnny Majors*

"The head coach must remain a little aloof from the players and, to a certain extent, from the coaches."
    - General Robert Neyland

"In the football business, if you're standing still, you're losing ground." *- Doug Dickey*

"Once they paint orange on you, it never washes off." *- Harvey Robinson, UT head football coach, 1953-54*

"What I wanted to do was try football (professionally in Canada). If it didn't work out, my plan was to start work immediately on baseball—go to Mexico...South America...wherever I needed to go, and work my way up. Of course, 13 years later I was still playing football." *-Condredge Holloway*

"It's not Neyland Stadium."
- Johnny Majors on the Louisiana Superdome in New Orleans

"Open the portals of the Rose Bowl, boys, there's a pretty fair country football team heading out that way, the Tennessee Volunteers."
- Joe Williams, New World Telegram, 1939

"We may have a "horse and buggy offense" but we've got a dashboard and a TV set added." *- Bowden Wyatt*

"It's a modern major miracle that we went through the season without having our goal line crossed or a field goal scored."
- General Robert Neyland, UT football coach, on his Volunteers' amazing unscored upon 1939 season—the last football team to achieve that feat

"They're good alright. They even look strong in the huddle." - *Jim Pittman, Tulane coach, on the #2 ranked, 1967 Vols*

"I walked in here and couldn't believe it. It was like we were playing at home." - *Peerless Price, on seeing the many Vol fans in Vanderbilt Stadium*

"He's raised everybody's play around him to another level because of his competitive spirit, ability and leadership."
- Phil Fulmer on Vol quarterback Peyton Manning

"Half of the time he's covered, he's still going to catch it."
- Steve Spurrier, Florida coach, on Carl Pickens, Vol receiver

"There is a happy union of the past, present, and future on autumn Saturdays, when Tennessee fans pour into the huge bowl...some of them literally rising out of the river via the fleet of yachts that dock less than 100 yards from the stadium, many of them shamelessly dressed in the bright orange and white that only the football team wore in simpler times." - *Ben Byrd*

"They're not going to beat us because their fans make a lot of noise..." - *Vinny Testaverde prior to his Miami Hurricanes being beaten 35-7 by the Vols*

"I saw all of these cars coming with orange flags on them and I thought Florida was coming to town. I'll never make that mistake again."
- *Hyatt Regency Chef, New Orleans*

"Personally, my greatest thrill at Tennessee was watching our 1967 team gathering itself after losing to UCLA in the opener and build a head of steam that lasted for nine games." *- Bob Johnson*

"I think if God wants something to happen, it's going to happen. I won't give luck the credit. I give the credit to God. He's standing up there right now, with Smokey next to him, wearing an orange jersey."
— Tee Martin, after defeating Arkansas in 1998

"We all remember the things we do in the Alabama game."
- Johnny Majors

"Sometimes you've just got to win ugly."
- Phil Fulmer, head football coach of the 1998 National Champion Vols

"For a Tennessee player, there is no better time to be a hero than the third Saturday in October."
     - Mike Strange, Knoxville News Sentinel

"Legend has it that boys grow into men in the span of one afternoon whenever the Vols meet the Tide."
     - Ben Byrd

"Lord, we are thankful we have gone this far. We hope each and every one of us can play this game as well as we did those of the past. We are thankful to be here and we pray we can win. Amen." *- Sam Bartholomew, captain, 1939 Tennessee football team, prior to taking the field in the 1940 Rose Bowl*

"The biggest thing that caused problems for me at Tennessee was not being able to beat Alabama and Auburn regularly." _- Bill Battle_

"I knew we were going to win the Arkansas game. I was trying to figure out how when their quarterback dropped the ball."
- Raynoch Thompson, subsequent to the Vols' 28-24 victory over the Hogs in 1998

"It is no doubt a cliché, yet true, that southern football is a religion."

- Willie Morris

Vanderbilt

"Who knows? Amid world beating hearts the tumult and shouting starts." *- Vanderbilt baseball player and renowned sportswriter, Grantland Rice*

"The central core of this institution, the reason we are here, is that we are an academic institution." *- Gordon Gee, Vanderbilt Chancellor*

"Due to its ingredients...courage, mental and physical condition, spirit and its terrific body contact which tends to sort the men from the boys...football remains one of the great games of all time." *- Grantland Rice*

"When you're hired, you're fired. The date just hasn't been put in." *- C.M. Newton*

"My special trouble is that I'm now head-coaching one of the teams that I'd want to play."
- Steve Sloan, Vanderbilt coach

"Our opportunity is to set high standards in terms of the student as athlete and...still perform well on the athletic playing field." *- Gordon Gee, Vanderbilt Chancellor*

"Don't live on the fading memories of your forefathers. Go out and make your own records, and leave some memories for others to live by." *- Dan McGugin, Vanderbilt head football coach*

"You take the ball, you put it in the proper position, and then you squeeze the ball until you hear the ball go, "pssshhhhhh.'"

- Lou Holtz, Notre Dame football coach, after his offense fumbled seven times against Vanderbilt in 1996, on the advice he has given ball carriers to avert such mistakes

"Football has one glaring weakness. The game is built largely on constant rule-breaking such as holding, offside, backs illegally in motion, pass interference and other factors that play a big, if illegal part in the results." *- Grantland Rice*

"Play for your own self-respect and the respect of your teammates." *- Dan McGugin*

"Men, those people in the stands out there haven't heard of Southern football. When they think about the South, they think about the Civil War--they think about pain, suffering and death. Many people have no idea of what southern manhood is all about. Today we can show them. When your mothers looked on you sleeping your cradles twenty years ago, they wondered when the time would come when you could bring honor to the South. That time has arrived!"
- *Dan McGugin, 1924, preparing his team to play Minnesota*

"HOW YOU FIGHT IS HOW YOU WILL BE REMEMBERED."
- *Dan McGugin*

"You are about to be put through an ordeal which will show the stuff that's in you. What a glorious chance you have!"
- *Coach Dan McGugin in 1921, addressing his undefeated Vanderbilt squad*

"...They have been waiting a long time, most of them. Finally, "Coach" has come home. Beloved, loyal, unselfish and considerate Coach McGugin. The same smile. Those Irish eyes of blue, so big and kindly. A lock of brown hair standing up in the breeze. Those same short steps...There is plenty of time in that better land of no defeats. Each day they will sit in the circle where the sun is always warm and the grass ever green. And when each Commodore comes out of the battle of life, just a bit weary, "Coach" will stand up, pat him on the back and welcome him to the squad that never dies."
  - The *Vandy Gold* website

"Winning isn't everything, it's the only thing."
- 1953 saying that is often attributed to Vandy Coach Red Sanders, according to Bartlett's Familiar Quotations, sixteenth edition (1992)

"With old-timers, whether it be baseball players or fighters, the ability to hit goes last." *- Grantland Rice*

"I felt like a Yankee and a stranger when I first came here, but I guess I've been reconstructed. Vanderbilt is the greatest thing that ever happened to me."
- Bob Werckle, 1951 All-American Offensive/Defensive Tackle

"...sort of a Rambo on a leash." *- Tennessean sports columnist Larry Woody's description of Vanderbilt All-American linebacker Chris Gaines*

"Sportsmanship should be the mortar of the athlete but never an entity in itself for conscious play."
- Grantland Rice

"Vanderbilt is the best team in the South and one of the best in the nation. No Southern team, recruited by any means, has classed with it. This team was secured by honest athletic methods. No inducements are held out for athletes to go to Vanderbilt. The team has been built up by methods above criticism and it proves one thing, that honesty pays in college athletics as well as elsewhere." - *Atlanta Journal, 1906*

"The worst mistake a coach can make is to get caught without material." - *Red Sanders*

"Hit em' hard and carry 'em to the ground. It reduces their enthusiasm."
- Dan McGugin

"I owe sport a great deal. Not only has it enabled me to make a comfortable living, it helped me grow up."
   - Grantland Rice

"It's not whether you win or lose, it's how you play the game."
   - Grantland Rice

"Kids in Texas are not impressed by each other's press clippings. They know each other too well."
   - Jess Neely

"As an integral part of a private research University and a charter member of the Southeastern Conference, we are committed to setting and achieving standards of excellence in education and athletics by developing the full potential of our student-athletes and staff. Individually and together, we are accountable for placing the highest value on people, integrity and winning."
- The Vanderbilt Commodore Mission Statement

"For when the Great Scorer comes,
    To write against your name,
He marks—not that you won or lost—
    But how you played the game."
- Grantland Rice

"The drama of sport is a big part of the drama of life and the scope of that drama is endless."

- Grantland Rice

A Tailgater's Guide to SEC Football

"A Tailgater's Guide To SEC Football: Traditions and History of the Southeastern Conference" is a recently published book by sports writer Chris Warner that celebrates the histories and colorful traditions of each Southeastern Conference institution.

"SEC football fans are passionate like no others," Warner said. "This book is dedicated to all the southern people who live for Saturdays in the fall, for those individuals who plan their business and personal engagements around their favorite team's football schedule, and to those who just can't get enough of the SEC.

The 256-page book contains a comprehensive history of the game of football in the South including chapters on each of the SEC schools highlighting their unique history and traditions; greatest players and coaches; mascots, alma maters and fight songs; and more. The book's foreword was written by former all-around LSU and SEC great, and three-time All-American, Tommy Casanova.

"A Tailgater's Guide To SEC Football" features the best places to eat and drink before the game in each town. Also included are twelve new recipes for tailgaters from the kitchen of Chris Warner's brother, Jeff Warner, a Cajun chef who works in Manhattan, New York.

Price: $19.95 + $2.00 S&H

SEND TO: CEW Enterprises, P.O. Box 44189, Capitol Station, Baton Rouge, LA 70804-4189

SEC Baseball History & Tradition

"SEC Baseball History & Tradition" is the second in a trilogy of published books by sports writer Chris Warner on the many colorful histories and traditions of each baseball program in the Southeastern Conference.

In addition to chapters related to each of the SEC member institutions' baseball programs (profiles of great players and coaches, stadiums, etc.), the 224-page book contains a history of the game of baseball in America, as well as a comprehensive section on the College World Series in Omaha, Nebraska. In the CWS section, readers will find a thorough history of the event and Rosenblatt Stadium, as well as what to do while you are in Omaha for the annual College World Series.

The book's foreword was written by former LSU Tiger second baseman, and CWS hero, Warren Morris.

Price: $15.95 + $2.00 S&H

SEND TO: CEW Enterprises, P.O. Box 44189, Capitol Station, Baton Rouge, LA 70804-4189

SEC Basketball History & Tradition

"SEC BASKETBALL HISTORY & TRADITION" is the third title of a trilogy of books by sports writer Chris Warner that celebrates the unique histories and colorful traditions of each Southeastern Conference school. The foreword of the book is written by former LSU player Ricky Blanton, the afterword is with former LSU head basketball coach Dale Brown, and the middle of the book contains a "Tribute to Pete Maravich," the greatest scorer in the history of the college game.

"This book is for anyone who loves basketball," Warner said. "It is a comprehensive look at the sport in the Southeastern Conference-its humble beginnings on the campuses prior to the turn of the century, and the many changes that have transpired and altered the game over the course of the last thirty years."

The 256-page book contains a history of basketball in America, including chapters on each of the SEC schools highlighting their unique hardwood history and traditions; arenas, greatest players and coaches; mascots, and more!

Price: $17.95 + $2.00 S&H

SEND TO: CEW Enterprises, P.O. Box 44189, Capitol Station, Baton Rouge, LA 70804-4189